Brave
in a
New World

A Guide to Grieving

YVONNE BROADY

Edited by Yvonne Renee Lucas
Illustrated by Karla Leaphart
Photography by Joan Siegel-Torres

ISBN: 978-1-4834-2229-9 (sc)
ISBN: 978-1-4834-2231-2 (hc)
ISBN: 978-1-4834-2230-5 (e)

Library of Congress Control Number: 2014920942

Lulu Publishing Services rev. date: 12/10/2014

This book is dedicated to the memory of my
husband, Clarence Cortez Loftin III.

Chuck, you will remain in my heart forever. I am so
blessed to have had you in my life. You were truly a unique
individual, my dream guy … a man for all seasons.

CONTENTS

PREFACE

It was December 27, 2007, at 4:30 in the afternoon, two days after Christmas, one day before my life would change forever. My husband had been ill on Christmas day, and actually, I thought he had caught a virus that I had contracted two weeks earlier. Chuck was so sick on that day that he didn't get up from bed to have Christmas dinner. I still suspected the flu. He had been to the doctor, and the doctor said that it was the flu, but I was also aware that he didn't seem to have any cold symptoms. He wasn't sneezing or coughing, but at that point, I still wasn't alarmed.

The morning after Christmas, I woke up and noticed that my husband suddenly looked like skin and bones. I immediately called the doctor, and he scheduled a CAT scan. Chuck had the scan on December 26, and the doctor called me the next day. When I answered the phone, he said he was glad that I had picked up the phone so he could speak to me first, then he'd speak to my husband. The doctor told me he had seen something on Chuck's pancreas. He said that he would have to do a biopsy. I nearly flipped. I couldn't believe my ears for I knew the seriousness of what the doctor was saying. After he spoke to me, he then spoke to my husband. Chuck and I both cried—and I literally screamed.

The next few weeks were like a fog. We decided to try an alternative method of treatment as we awaited the arrival of the biopsy date. Chuck began to lose more weight with the holistic treatment, and after the formal diagnosis of "yes, it is pancreatic cancer" and "yes, it is in the head of the pancreas" (which is the worst location for pancreatic cancer to be found) and "yes, it is stage four," we decided to go for more traditional treatment at Sloan-Kettering Hospital in New York City. Our oncologist was compassionate, knowledgeable, and willing to work with us as we proceeded forward with hope for a miracle. She never dashed our hopes.

In the ensuing weeks and months, my husband prayed, kept a journal, and never complained. He had good days in the beginning, and we were encouraged on a few occasions, but as time went on, the chemotherapy took its toll, and eventually, he became so weak that the effects became more of a minus than a plus. Chuck was still not eating well, just small morsels of food, which were all he could get down. But we were thankful for the fact that he could just eat, because maintaining a balanced weight was critical for him to survive. We both prayed for that miracle, and I tried to be as normal as possible, not ever uttering a discouraging word. I saw my robust, athletic husband go from a strong, healthy man to a slow-moving, bald shadow of himself.

Chuck had great pride and dignity, and he did not want me to know how much pain he was in, so he didn't tell me. When I noticed him lying in an awkward position and asked if he was in pain, he would tell me I was being negative. He pushed as much as he could until finally the chemotherapy was beginning to have a deleterious effect, and he had to stop treatment.

I remember on the last day, he asked his oncologist, "So, there's nothing else you can do for me?" Oh, I thought my heart would break into little, teeny tiny pieces. My dear, sweet lifelong companion, my handsome husband who dressed so nattily in his tweeds and sweaters as he went to his treatment, was now faced with no more hope.

At one point during his chemotherapy treatments (I hadn't been for a while—my brother-in-law had been going with him, which gave me a bit of a break), the doctor called me into her office and said I was my husband's source of strength and that he was still alive because of me. She said I was his lifeline. My heart sank. When I came out of her office, Chuck was waiting for me down the corridor, and when he saw that I had been crying, he took my hand and comforted me. Our bond was what carried us through.

I did not go to the very last visit with his oncologist because I could not bear to be there and face the inevitable. It was the place where we had gone in the beginning with such hope, and now everything seemed so final.

Soon Chuck settled in with hospice care at home. We had the most wonderful nurses and tons of medications to treat the pain. The nurses were so kind to Chuck. He loved them too—probably more than me at times as I became the caregiver/taskmaster, and they were the angels of mercy.

Chuck endured many emergencies, numerous medications, and the slow deterioration of his body, but never his mind. Eventually, he was not able to get around on his own; he wasn't able to sit up or lie down or move his arms and legs. I found this to be the most unbelievable experience to have to witness. The unimaginable transformation of my dear husband as he went through this experience was beyond fathomable. He endured his fate with as much dignity as he could. He never cried out, and although he cried when I wasn't around, occasionally he would cry in front of me.

He would ask me to forgive him for having put me through this horrible ordeal. I assured him that it was not his fault and I could never blame him for this unreal, random circumstance. Sometimes he would feel cold and sometimes he would feel hot, and I just wanted to hold him and absorb some of his discomfort. I really just wanted to wake up from this nightmare. I wanted our life back.

On January 24, 2009, four days after the inauguration of Barack Obama, our first black president of the United States, my husband, Clarence Cortez Loftin III, who meant everything to me—my dream guy, my protector and provider, and the source of my strength—passed away peacefully at home at the age of 61. His anguish and pain were extinguished, and my painful journey was about to begin.

This book is meant to be a guide and source of inspiration and hope for those who are grieving the loss of a spouse. The process of grieving requires a conscious effort on the part of the griever. It's not to be taken lightly or haphazardly, but we must also know that it is a long and arduous process, and the only one who can get through it is the one who is left: the bereaved spouse.

This book is about being brave and courageous in a brand-new world. This is not meant to be a definitive guide on how to grieve, but I hope my experience will assist those who are grieving the loss of a spouse by illustrating what can be expected as one embarks on a grieving journey.

After years of marriage, no matter how few or how many, it is up to the grieving spouse to re-create a life for herself or himself. I hope this book helps to make that task easier.

Yvonne Broady

CHAPTER 1

My Journey: In the Beginning

There was so much to do after my husband passed away that I didn't have time to be present with myself. There were family members and friends swirling all around. There were funeral plans to make, an obituary to write, and a repast to organize. After the funeral, there were thank-you notes to write, estate matters to attend to, etc.

My only son, Karim, stayed with me for a week after my husband died. He subsequently came and spent the night on Wednesday of each week for a few months after, until I could become acclimated to living alone. This was the first time I would be living alone since 1976. And now, here it was 2009.

The morning that my husband passed away, family and friends came over. They cleaned out the bedroom by breaking down the hospital bed, getting rid of medications, and making up my bed. They really tried and succeeded in creating an atmosphere that was serene and void of the evidence of what had taken place just hours earlier.

I was in such a deep, murky, dark fog, but I knew that I didn't want my son to stay longer than the week. I had enough presence of mind to want to get on with grieving, whatever that would be like. Even though I was clueless as to what to expect, I wanted to get on with it.

It was frightening to be alone, especially at night, but I figured out ways to feel secure. I locked my bedroom door at night, I made sure the chain was on the entrance door, and I checked to make sure that my balcony door was locked securely. Then I prayed that I'd make it till morning. Night was not my friend during the early stages of my loss. To make sure that I felt secure in my bed, I would stuff the bed with three pillows that I could cuddle with. This helped me to not feel so alone and made the bed feel less empty.

I drank teas to make me sleep, keep me calm, make me less anxious, and give me more energy. I cried and cried and cried until I could hardly see. I was blinded by a wall of tears. With no need to be the strong one, I let it flow until the next moment when tears would flow and flow again. I dispensed with stringent standards or expectations. I knew I needed to grieve the way I felt and wanted to, and I could not let anyone else's discomfort with my tears dictate my mourning. So I withdrew and grieved deeply for my husband and for myself, on my own terms.

The prospect of waking up every day and being faced with the same reality was very exhausting to me. I just wanted this to be over. At night, I would go to bed and pull the covers up over my head and hope that I would sleep for several hours, only to be met with the same reality of another day without Chuck.

Every day seemed to move in slow motion, and the days turned into endless weeks, but I was able to accomplish the tasks that needed to be done. I decided to begin going through my husband's belongings almost immediately. If I waited, I was afraid I might not be able to deal with sorting all the clothes, books, college degrees, personal items, and things one accumulates when he or she is alive. I'm glad that I tackled this daunting task early on; it helped to clear space for me to begin my life afresh, although I had no idea it would be a byproduct of this undertaking.

So, daily I sorted, called charities, arranged pickups, arranged for items that would go to family members, etc. At times, I felt the need to leave certain things in a particular way in case he "came back" or as an attempt to honor his memory. Some items I left alone, tucking them away or leaving them in place, just in case he was to "come back". Sorting pictures was another unbearable task—it was so heartbreaking to look at pictures. But in some odd way, I felt that my husband had suffered so greatly during his illness, that my looking at the pictures, no matter how painful, would somehow counterbalance everything he had gone through.

Then there was the issue with my appetite; I could not eat. Chuck hadn't been able to eat much during his illness. His appetite was really compromised, and it was critical for him to keep his weight up as he went through chemotherapy. After he passed away, I lost my desire to eat. On some level, I felt that not eating was almost a way of honoring him. After all, he couldn't eat, so why should I enjoy a meal? Eventually, my eating habits improved, but it was a while before that happened.

I created a prayerful, meditative routine and practiced it daily, usually early in the morning before I started my day. My moods were generally the same in the beginning: feelings of immeasurable loss, sorrow, and brokenheartedness. Some days, the waves of emotion literally took my breath away. I longed to see my husband again, just one last time. I wanted to talk to him and tell him things I never really got the chance to say.

I had all sorts of emotions early on. First I felt guilty that maybe I could've been more patient at times. I felt angry with God and screamed and ranted at Him: "How could you have done this terrible thing to my husband and me? You destroyed my family, God. How could You?"

After all, Chuck was my *dream guy* … and now that dream had been unexpectedly shattered by an incredibly villainous, cruel, unanticipated, deadly disease. How unfair!

After the funeral, when I was no longer surrounded by people, my emotions began to settle into a kind of "non-feeling state." I felt numb, as though I was in a fog. Then I began to feel a kind of nervousness, a sort of unbalance. As I walked, I felt uneasy, as if I could easily fall down. The uncertainty in my step reflected the fact that I didn't feel safe or secure. It was the feeling of having lost my footing, as if I were about to fall off the earth and into the bottom of the ocean. My life meant nothing without my husband in it—I was virtually holding on for dear life.

The whole experience seemed like a crazy occurrence, and I was in an unusual state of being: neither here nor there, but completely and utterly alone. This was the beginning, and I call this Stage One: Numbness. I was somewhere between heaven and earth, a kind of grief limbo. Sometimes I would walk back and forth in my apartment just to keep myself aware and to feel alive. I would sit and cry and cry and cry. I would smell my husband's clothes. Chuck had a very distinct scent: it was sweet and lovely. His scent lingered on his hats, handkerchiefs, gloves, and other items that he'd worn. I would smell them every day. Then I would touch his keys and look at things that just a few weeks earlier he had touched or worn.

Every day was gray, even if the sun was shining. Every day seemed lifeless and still and without a beginning or an end. The days became a stream of time. I went to bed and drank a cup of Sleepytime tea, and rubbed Bath and Body Works Sleep lotion into my wrist, only to awaken and continue where I'd left off: crying—sometimes wailing— empty and in pain.

Chuck had been everything to me: my best friend, husband, and confidant. He had become a part of me, and now half of me had vanished … just like that! I yearned to be with him in heaven, which is where, according to my belief system and faith, I felt he was. I wanted to soar to where Chuck was in that limitless place called heaven. My heart ached for him, and the pain was excruciating. These constant waves of feelings were very exhausting, and I could not foresee an ending to this new way of being. Every day was the same. I could count on pain and sorrow greeting me when I awoke, and then accompanying me until it was time to sleep. It was my new normal.

I stayed in touch with my family physician, who knew my husband and me from the time we were first married, through Chuck's illness, and beyond. Dr. Richard Shepherd was so great and offered all kinds of medical advice to help me feel comfortable and get through the days ahead. But one day, I awoke and knew that I needed more help. Now mind you, I am blessed with many friends and a wonderful family, but this experience was one where—as the bereaved one—I knew I had to forge this journey alone. "*You* are the only one who can go through this," my friend Kathy told me, and she was so right.

The organization that had provided hospice services for my husband said they could provide one-on-one counseling at my home. This was great as I felt safe at home and didn't want to travel to another borough. By this time, I was ready to talk to someone who would listen to my tale of sorrow, loss, and incredible pain without saying a word. Although I did not know it then, my daily healing rituals and the opportunity to open up to someone would help me get through each painful day until eventually, I began to slowly feel a little better.

This would be a long time coming because so many things reminded me of Chuck's absence. The scent of a flower, a whiff of cologne, seeing someone on the street I would mistake for Chuck, a note in his handwriting that dropped out of a book, or just a memory that crept into my thoughts every now and then. Finally, I learned to go with the flow and not beat myself up for feelings that I had every day. I slowly felt that I was moving in the right direction, and I felt fortunate to have people in my life who would help me adjust.

CHAPTER 2

My Journey: Help!

lthough I've experienced the loss of relatives over the years, the most devastating event for me was the death of my father in 2005. Chuck was such a great support to me during that time as we all gathered together to honor my dad, Samuel Carlyle Broady. When Chuck passed away, my family did what we do: we came together to make preparations for my husband's funeral. This was done with precision and great organization. My two brothers, Anthony and Emil, and my sister, Marie, came and organized everything from the funeral service to the repast. Chuck's funeral service was beautiful, and I felt proud of how we were able to create a fitting tribute to him. Now, I was left grieving for the very person who had been my support when I needed him most, and I had no one I could lean on dearly other than myself. But how does one do that, when you feel like a shadow of yourself?

Having reached out for counseling, I found a wonderful person who came to my home once a week. I looked forward to seeing her, and we immediately established a trust and bond as I told my story—my life with Chuck, his illness, and my continued sorrow. She helped me begin to put things in perspective. We eventually added a spiritual/ religious element to the counseling that helped me move forward with my grieving. She would sit on my couch; I would sit in my green chair or in Chuck's leather reclining chair. She would listen, and I would talk and weep. Her counsel helped me move through the tunnel of despair I was in.

As we continued our sessions, I began to feel a bit closer to the light that I still could not see. During this period, I decided to also seek pastoral counseling. The wonderful pastor from my church who officiated at my husband's funeral service was my choice. The Rev. Dr. Arnold Isidore Thomas came to see me two days after my husband passed away to gather information for the service and comfort my spirit. Although he'd never met him, he was able to create a sermon that captured the essence of who my husband Clarence C. Loftin III was. In fact, many who attended the service were convinced that he had known him.

So, Dr. Thomas became my choice to visit when I felt I needed to talk. He was wonderful. He listened to me as I cried, and I asked him many "why" questions: Why did he have to die? Why did this have to happen? Where is my husband now? Is he in heaven? Where is heaven? How can I go on? Why did God do this to us—to Chuck, to me, and my little family?

Dr. Thomas gave me a new way of tackling the "why" questions, and he encouraged me to grieve. He was a great source of solace and spiritual sustenance during this time. The combination of these two resources—individual and pastoral counseling—would form the foundation for my being able to begin the process of putting my life back together, but in a new way.

As weeks went on, I began to feel like I was becoming a bit stronger. It was now three months since my husband's passing, and I hadn't been away from New York City, which had become my epicenter of pain, loss, and sorrow. So I decided that a brief trip might do me a world of good. I chose to go someplace close and stay in a hotel so I could still be near friends and relatives who were near and dear to me. I planned to take a trip to Washington, DC, where I have both friends and family.

As I was preparing to go, I began to feel nervous and tense, even fearful. My train tickets were purchased. I booked a beautiful room in a five-star hotel near the White House and the National Mall, and I was looking forward to my trip. Then suddenly, I began to feel anxious about it all. I called a friend who suggested that I see a physician who was also an acupuncturist. I was keen on this idea particularly since I was reluctant to go the traditional route and use prescription drugs to keep me calm. I visited the acupuncturist/physician, and after the first session, I was able to leave town. This was truly a miracle since I would normally have been petrified of having acupuncture and also because I was just about to cancel the trip altogether and lose major money.

The trip was of great value. I ended up taking several trips that first year, and it always felt good to get away and be coddled and loved by friends and family. The change of routine, the different environment, and the stepping away from the mourning space helped to relieve me of the sorrow and sadness that followed me daily. I felt as though I was evolving, but the path seemed slow, and I wasn't quite sure when I would ever be done grieving. I began to think maybe I would never be done with it. I was in murky water trying to swim, but not sure if I could save myself from the thoughts, memories, sense of loss, and the inability to see a bright future without my husband in it. It was a very scary time for me. Now, eight months had passed, and my progress seemed minimal.

In the meantime, I decided that I might benefit from being in a bereavement group. So in between many mini vacations, I contacted Sloan-Kettering Hospital where my husband had been treated for his cancer, and they set up an appointment for me to come in for an interview. This would be the first time that I was heading back to where my husband had gone weekly for his chemo and doctor visits.

When I arrived, I was interviewed by the bereavement group facilitator and social worker. After telling her my story from beginning to end, she said I would be a great addition to the group they were forming. I would be in a group with men and women who had lost their spouses to various forms of cancer and had all been treated at Sloan-Kettering.

The bereavement group lasted ten weeks. Each session was one and a half hours. In the very beginning, one and a half hours was long enough for me, but toward the middle as the bond within the group became stronger, one and a half hours wasn't enough time to say all I wanted to say. The group consisted of two men and six women. We were all different except for that singular event that altered each and every one of our lives forever: the loss of a spouse from cancer. But the way we bonded transcended any physical differences of age, color, religion, or race. It was the humanity of it all. We shared an experience that had left us with a deep sense of loss, a tremendous depth of sadness, and a sense of feeling alone—all alone—in a strange, new world.

Our group facilitator guided us through each session as we all told our stories. We listened as each story usually began with the diagnosis and ended with the passing. As the weeks went on, we learned about the lives of our spouses, their relationship with their families, and the seasons of their lives. The bonding happened unexpectedly for me and probably for all of us. We found ourselves sharing thoughts and questions that we could never have shared with anyone else who wasn't tackling his or her own grief. As time went on, I felt that I knew each person very well. I knew about their families, children, lifestyles—the whole lot—and they learned about mine.

We had rules of conduct. We'd listen to each person tell his or her story without interrupting. Ultimately, we were able to talk about everything. And as each narrative was repeated and repeated and repeated, we listened without interrupting again and again and again. One day, someone asked, "Does anyone believe in the supernatural?" Some of us raised our hands. This began a discussion that some of us felt strongly about.

We discussed whether or not one could continue a relationship with a spouse even though that person was no longer alive. We wondered aloud about some of the signs and signals that would let us know that our spouse was still with us. Some of us were believers and some were not. We shared stories of feeling like we were being hugged, flickering lights, a sensation of being tucked into bed at night. The stories we shared we could never talk about with anyone except us. Those of us who had never experienced such events just listened, but we never pooh-poohed or judged what anyone shared as wishful thinking or crazy or not real.

While I was in the bereavement group, we talked about many topics, including dating. I was not even thinking about dating, although several people had mentioned to me that sooner or later, if I decided to explore new relationships, it would be what my husband would want for me. We talked about being lonely and alone and the possibility of dating and intimacy. The initial thought of a first date, however, was rather creepy and strange and not anything I saw myself doing, at least not at that point.

We brought in pictures, and we pored over photos of family gatherings, children, grandchildren, good times, wedding pictures, stories of our lives, the way we lived ... the lives we led with our spouses. We were respectful of each other: loving, empathetic and kind, patient and caring. We cried with each other and for each other. And we mourned for each other and for ourselves. But most of all, we felt safe and protected by each other's recognition of our individual fragility and our woeful state of being, as we shared our journey stories and our feelings.

I found my experience with my bereavement group to play a pivotal part in moving me through the grieving process. In a sad, strange way, the knowledge that I was not alone was a comfort. I didn't have to be strong; I didn't have to be quiet. I could just be.

CHAPTER 3

The Firsts

When Chuck died, my whole world—as I had known it—ended, and a new one began. It felt like I had just emerged, newly born on the planet. It was as if I had lost a part of my body (my heart really) and now I was standing, teeter-tottering like an infant taking its first steps. I refer to this period as Stage Three: Teeter-Totter. I was actually experiencing Stages 1, 2, and 3 all at once! But I'm getting ahead of myself. I will explain the stages of the grief experience in a later chapter.

Many things seemed new. Joy had left my body and my soul; nothing made me happy or seemed funny. I kept seeing the sadness in so many things. No longer could I watch tragic incidents on the news or experience anything upsetting. Although I was never a big fan of violent TV shows or news reports, I developed a heightened sensitivity to all things violent and destructive.

As the first year wore on, I was also about to experience what I call, "The Firsts." These were the initial milestones that I had to experience and move through. The *first* month after his death, the *first* wedding anniversary without him here, the *first* time we weren't together on his birthday, the *first* Christmas, and so on.

By the time the first summer arrived, I made attempts to become more social and began traveling in and out of town quite a bit. I always felt a *bit* better as I traveled out of town, usually by train, to places far but near. Everyone I encountered during this period—my family, my brother, cousins, and dear friends—was very kind, gracious, helpful, and hospitable, and I began to feel more in touch with myself. Although I wasn't consciously aware of it, I was shaking off that feeling of numbness, and I could see a pinhole of light at the end of the tunnel—a very tiny dot of light, but it was there.

The first Thanksgiving, the first Christmas, my first birthday without him, and that first New Year's Eve were all big events for me as I was acutely aware of my husband's absence. The Fourth of July, which we rarely celebrated, became a first, too. There was also that first visit to the gravesite. Since my husband's funeral on that snowy day in January 2009, I was never able to gain the strength and courage to visit the place where he had been laid to rest.

Some or most of the people in my bereavement group had been to their spouses' grave sites several times, but I had not made the trip back. In my mind and heart, it had become the obstacle I needed to overcome in order to move ahead. The longer I waited, the more anxious I felt inside. I shared this with my bereavement group, and they never judged me. Actually, they made suggestions as to how I could decrease my anxiety. They understood.

So on Chuck's birthday, July 11, 2009, I made my way to his gravesite. Seeing his name on the crypt gave me mixed emotions— surprise, sadness, and comfort. I took a picture of the crypt. I prayed and I felt the presence of Chuck's spirit. Then I began to think about how my husband had been so proud to have purchased the plots where he and I could be buried. He felt that this was a great accomplishment, and so, I felt it would be wrong to not visit. That sunny, hot day in July was a good day, and I felt that I had reached a milestone and overcome a hurdle.

When I went back to my bereavement group and mentioned that I had visited my husband's grave site, everyone was so happy for me. They knew that overcoming that obstacle was huge. I was glad that I had my group, now my friends.

I continued with my acupuncture, which really helped to take the edge off and alleviate the tension that I was experiencing now and again. I also found peace and comfort in my friends. I had so many wonderful people around me: a loving family, and super-duper friends. Mostly, everyone remained close without hovering. This worked for me. I knew I could call on many, but ultimately, I was the only one who could pull myself out of this dismal place. No one could do it for me. I had to heal myself.

Something that helped me immensely was having a regular ritual with friends. I began to meet with friends for lunches, dinners, and cocktails. Sometimes I would even invite my friends over—not often, but more than never. I would make a specialty drink—a margarita, a Cosmo, or a lemon drop martini. We'd chat and laugh and have fun. Then one day, for the first time, I realized I was actually laughing a bit more, and before I knew it, the light at the end of the tunnel, that pinhole of light, was beginning to get larger.

Meeting with the girls every week after church on Wednesdays also became a part of my healing. My church held a regular Wednesday church service, and I had started going, ironically, while my husband was in the throes of his illness. I found the extra day of worship of great solace to me; it felt good to listen to God's Word. It helped to soothe my spirit as I wished and prayed for God's miracle of spontaneous healing for my husband. If I missed Sunday services, I felt I still had a chance to hear the Word and feel God's strength and love according to my own belief in the God of my understanding.

So during this period after Wednesday service, I would meet some girlfriends—sometimes two or three or one—and we would go somewhere to chat, eat, and drink cocktails. We laughed and joked and cried and prayed. We talked about our lives, our losses, our children, and about meeting men and gaining joy. Being with my girlfriends was a support that extended the grace in my Wednesday ritual at Space for Grace at the Riverside Church in New York City.

I began to feel better and not so zoned out. It was a gradual, positive step toward improving my arrested development. I felt uplifted, encouraged, and protected by the generosity of spirits, the sweetness and kindness, the encouragements, the silence, the listening, the laughter, and the tears that I shared with my girlfriends on these Wednesdays after church. Brenda, Donna, Lisa, Sabrina, and others helped to push me forward toward mental wellness and hope.

Then one day in early fall, that year of my great loss, I actually saw the light at the end of the tunnel become even brighter! Sunny days seemed sunnier (and not gray). I began to know that I could stay alive, and I didn't have to become an emotional zombie, a walking wounded in a world that was constantly blurred by my tears and my "Firsts." Without realizing it, I was now experiencing Stage Five: Reawakening.

CHAPTER 4

Forging a Life of My Own

When you're in a state of grief—suspended in times past and present, not able to move forward—you'll find that it is an unsettling place to be.

When my husband passed away, I knew that I was about to enter a new experience. As I mourned, I had to figure out how I would continue to exist on the planet without him. The fact that I had lived without a husband before I met Chuck had no impact on my present thoughts, as I was now twenty or so years older than that bygone era. I was now reawakening in a new world with new sets of rules and ways of being. Whoosh! Here I was, catapulted into a new existence, suspended in the air of my own thoughts and fears. I found that I had to compartmentalize my thoughts. Grief overshadowed everything; on a computer, it would be compared to being the wallpaper on my desktop.

I began to think about how I looked, how I wanted to be, my own health, what my purpose in life would be, and how I could fulfill my destiny, whatever I discovered that to be. So, I prayed and meditated daily. I asked God to help me know the things that were pressing on my heart. I also continued my social activities with friends and healing rituals with professionals. I sorted through Chuck's belongings and eventually stopped when I knew I had done all I could do. I decided to re-create my living space in a way that was comfortable for me. I didn't want to be surrounded by sad memories. I wanted my home to be a place where I felt safe and secure, and ultimately, I wanted it to be a healing sanctuary for my mind, body, heart, and soul.

I began to eat differently and found myself losing many pounds. I began to feel stronger and more in control of myself as I went from looking sallow and feeling weak to feeling stronger and looking healthier. I wanted to survive my circumstance and live and thrive—not become a recluse or become ill or vanish.

I did all this and more. I maintained a journal and read books on grieving and being a widow. I had to somehow organize my thoughts as I went through the process of creating a new life. It went something like this: I had a metaphorical box for spiritual modalities, a box for transformative practices for the mind, body, and spirit. I had a box for thinking about and searching for my purpose. I had a box for healing my mind and heart in ways suggested by my healing mentors. I had an imaginary box for restorative assistance, such as pastoral, group, and individual counseling. I had a box to stop, breathe, and take stock—to relax and just be. Oh, and one last box was for me to allow myself to cry, cry, cry, or to walk back and forth in my apartment in disbelief, or to weep uncontrollably as I smelled my husband's clothes and felt him close by.

Daily I prayed and meditated for direction and guidance that I might know what God wanted me to do. I often wondered, "If everyone has a purpose, what is mine?" But most importantly, I thanked God. In the midst of my feelings of loss, despair, brokenheartedness, and instability, yes, I thanked God. I thanked Him for my life, which was better than most, and for my husband, because even though he was no longer here, I was grateful we had known each other and had the opportunity to build a life together. I thanked God for my son and for my siblings and for my incredible parents. I thanked God for my lovely home filled with anything I could ever need or want, and for my amazing friends, who were all different, but always there for me.

I actually thought about whether I should start working again, but that thought came and went in a flash. Eventually, I was able to look at my life as a clean slate, starting from scratch. The sky was the limit … sort of.

I also tried to keep up with my own health. I took to veggie juicing. I created juices for the pancreas, anxiety, depression, colds, flu, and diabetes (I don't even have diabetes, but I wasn't taking any chances). I felt so fragile that I feared any germ would latch onto me, take hold, and whisk me away. It was a strange, weird, and frightening time. Sometimes I felt like I was very shaky as I walked, and I felt as though I needed to be supported by walls on either side of me as I made my way through each new, long day.

My doctor, Dr. Richard Shepard, was so great. I would go into his office, and he was always available, accommodating, gracious, and kind. He would look at every boo-boo, treat every sneeze, and he would say nothing as I sat on the table swinging my legs, eyes tearing, longing for words to describe how I felt. His nurse, Janice, would literally cry with me and laugh as we remembered my husband who was funny, serious, warm, and prickly.

One day, my doctor looked at me as I cried and said, "I can't imagine what it's like to feel like your heart has been ripped right out of your chest." And that was a perfect description of how I'd been feeling. I was so brokenhearted. It was during this period that I sought an alternative health-care professional and, after careful research and consultation, I found a wonderful acupuncturist. Now, I am not a person to welcome having a bunch of needles placed in my skin, but I was so depressed and unwilling to take traditional antidepressants, I thought this might be a better course of action to follow to treat what I now knew was depression.

As I said earlier, the days seemed so gray after Chuck passed away. Each day—whether it was actually sunny, snowy, or cloudy—seemed like it streamed together as the same dreary, gray, and lifeless day after day after day. Eventually, I came to know that something was wrong. I began to feel like I could not lift myself out of this gloomy, constant state of despondency. I knew I needed extra help. So, upon recommendation from a friend, I decided to see a doctor who was a general practitioner and an acupuncturist.

When I went to see the acupuncturist one evening, I could hardly walk. I was planning to go out of town on my first trip since my husband had passed. However, as the trip got closer, I was on the brink of canceling because I felt unsure, nervous, and anxious. I knew I needed help. Dr. Lee explained to me that in Chinese medicine, there is such a thing as brokenhearted syndrome where one is so despondent that it feels as if one's heart is broken. He tested my Vitamin D level and made recommendations based on the blood test results. He also gave me my first acupuncture treatment. I remember that I was so out of it, I just said, "Okay," and laid on the table, surprisingly unafraid. He said he would be treating me for anxiety and depression. The first session worked so well that I was able to take my little trip and escape my crazy life in New York.

After a while, I found myself socializing a bit more, organizing girls' nights out, meeting friends for lunch or breakfast, and having occasional drinks with one or two friends at home. However, unbeknownst to anyone, I always felt so completely and utterly alone. Throughout everything I did, I found myself no longer feeling numb, but alone …

acutely alone! I missed my husband still, but I knew that I had to continue through the motions of survival, so I continued my spiritual rituals, seeing friends, and getting healthy while simultaneously mourning and crying my heart out. My friends called me brave. It was a while before I was able to label myself that.

For nearly a year after my loss, I saw myself as still married. I wore my wedding band and felt connected to Chuck. I had two lives: one foot was in my past life with my husband, while the other was in the here and now. It was a peculiar duality that became me until further notice.

The year wore on, and now I was faced with a new set of benchmarks that I previously referred to as the Firsts. During this period, my husband's mother, who'd suffered from Alzheimer's for nearly fourteen years, passed away. When I saw my husband's family during that time, I felt such a bond, and we got right back into the family swing of things, although their family had been diminished by two. But it's the way of life—the order of things—a new world ever changing, ever evolving. I felt sorrow for them having lost a brother, uncle, nephew, and a mom, sister, grandmother, all in the span of a year. I felt sadness for myself, too.

I began to think about when Chuck and I first got together and how our two families got along so well. My family bonded with my husband's family, and we had great fun together whenever we were around each other—laughing, telling jokes, a whoopin' and a hollerin'. I loved it when my husband's family would tell stories about when he was a boy, and I wanted to listen to them over and over again. I never ceased to delight in these tales and felt lucky to be a part of such a fine, extended family. We were just brothers and sisters. My brothers felt the same way; there was no in-law thing, just family all together as one.

That November up to New Year's Eve, I got through the Christmas season with the support of family and friends. New Year's was particularly important to me because it meant leaving the old year, the year my husband had been briefly alive and had passed. I would no longer be able to say, "Chuck just said that a year ago", or, "My husband just told me that a few weeks ago", and so on. In 2009, I could still say Chuck watched the inauguration of President Barack Obama on TV in January.

Now, I was entering 2010, and he was not alive to experience any of it. I would be entering a new year from day one, alone and on my own. My friends knew that I would be experiencing the first New Year's Eve without my husband, and some of them came back to my home that night after we had attended a gathering at another location. They sat with me, eating and laughing until the wee hours of the morning. They never realized how they helped to ease me into a new phase of my life.

So here we were in January 2010, and the first anniversary of Chuck's passing was approaching fast. For me, this was beyond symbolism. It was scary, but it would be somewhat liberating as well. The day arrived, a cold day in late January, and I visited my husband's grave. I sat by his crypt and prayed and wept and then sat in silence. It was a cold, wintry day, just like the day he was buried there, but the mausoleum was beautiful, and I felt at peace there. Soon after, I felt a shift and found that the light at the end of the tunnel was even a little bit brighter than before.

That year, I found myself out and about making new friends and staying connected with old ones. I became a little more active in my church. I became involved in events and causes that I found close to my heart. I still thought of Chuck every day, but I was able to tuck him away in my heart and *live*. I was *alive*! It was a slow and subtle process, but I was feeling alive.

I am aware that mourning for someone is relative to one's situation, so my evolution in the grieving process may seem shorter than most or longer than some, but grieving is a personal experience. No time limits, just all the time that one needs. It was a little over one year, and I was beginning to feel a *bit* better. I realized that I had to live in the present moment. I had to let each day be enough.

I managed to be brave and create a new life full of the things that were most meaningful to me: culture, the arts, music, faith, hope, and charity. I did it on my own, and with a little help from my friends, I had managed to step out of the tunnel, off of the curb, and into the light. I was no longer making my life manageable and safe; it was a process. Here are the steps I took toward my recovery:

1. Prayer and faith in the God of my understanding
2. Individual bereavement counseling
3. Group counseling
4. Socializing with friends
5. Healing rituals: prayer, meditation, church, yoga and exercise, talks with God, talks with my husband, and most importantly, silence
6. Re-creating my home so that I could live comfortably and mindfully surrounded by the things that have meaning for me
7. Eating healthy
8. Being grateful

CHAPTER 5

We Become Them

My husband was a rather complicated man. I like to refer to him as complicated yet simple. With Chuck, you always knew where you stood. He was very straightforward, and things were either black or white … no gray. I was the one who could see all sides of a situation, while my husband was what I would characterize as the *heavy*. I was the nice one; he, on the other hand, didn't suffer fools gladly. Chuck was very direct and did not beat around the bush. He never couched his words gently unless he was in a position where he had to be a mediator or diplomatic. In some circumstances, he could be harsh, a bit insensitive, and dogmatic. But at other times, he could be gracious, kind, generous, sympathetic, helpful, and sweet.

After Chuck passed away, I felt like I was at the mercy of everyone. It was my own sense of having lost my footing and feeling exposed, unprotected, and vulnerable. When Chuck was alive, I felt that I was under his protection. I knew I had an ally and a best friend who possessed the qualities and characteristics that I did not. And although I was happy as myself, his character or personality was a good balance to my own. I felt stronger with him than without him. I benefited from who he was, and he benefited from who I was—yin and yang.

But a strange thing occurred on my grieving journey, and it was subtle and gradual. I found myself beginning to feel bolder. I wasn't afraid to speak my mind, to say what I did and didn't prefer, to not go along to get along. I found myself criticizing and offering opinions and not caring about being the sweet, nice person anymore. I wanted people to know where I stood and what was acceptable to me and what wasn't. I didn't want to be taken advantage of. I didn't want people saying things to me that were hurtful or that I found unacceptable or offensive.

Then one day, I realized that I had become my husband in a strange, transformational, and beautiful way. I began to feel less vulnerable, and I had a new inner strength. I began to think about this odd change in me and came to the conclusion that I now embodied some of my husband's attributes and characteristics. It was like a gift, a legacy he had left for me. I had found my voice, a sort of self-protection against those things I feared. It was a new way of being a whole person so I could deal with life going forward. I had become him.

I do believe that part of grieving is to become one with the grief, and in doing so, a person examines every change that takes place within one's self. Of course for me, this self-realization was discovered over the course of time, many months into my process. Ultimately, I was grateful. I could stand in the truth of who I was now, possessing the best qualities of us both. I could go forth and be who I would be in the near and present future. I now discovered that I possessed the qualities I had been missing. The same aspects of his character that had kept my husband strong, were now keeping me safe, confident, and secure.

If a person pays attention, he or she will see that a spouse can continue to give you gifts that will sustain you for the long haul. They live on through the legacy they've left us. Yes, I believe we become them.

CHAPTER 6

The Supernatural

There's something peculiar about death, but unless you have actually witnessed the passing of someone, you can't imagine the eerie silence that follows and surrounds the space where the person breathed their last breath. It's an odd moment where you feel suspended in a timeless space, full of sadness, wonder, and a strange feeling of expectancy.

When my husband passed away, I awoke to complete silence. Not a sound or movement from him. But when I looked at my husband as he lay in the hospital bed next to our bed at home, I had this sense that he was no longer in his body. I came to believe that his body was just a shell, a costume that he had worn throughout his life. It was his human costume.

I didn't feel, as I had heard some people say, that his presence was still in the room. I felt nothing. But later as I reflected on that day, I remembered that a few odd things occurred. The lights in my apartment began flickering, and bulbs kept going out. These small events were not noticeable at first, but mere annoyances. I couldn't figure out why the lightbulbs kept blowing, especially at that time when the dark was not my friend. As time went on, these occurrences became more and more noticeable.

It was after several weeks and many lightbulb changes later that it occurred to me that this was not just about light bulbs blowing out. There seemed to be a pattern as if something or someone was trying to get my attention. I soon came to wonder if Chuck was somehow letting me know he was near and trying to give me comfort. Unfortunately, it was rather unnerving at first, and the fact that these strange occurrences seemed to happen at night, when I was most vulnerable and a little afraid, did not help matters much.

There were incidents of my dining room fan coming on by itself and lights dimming on their own. It was very unsettling at the least and astounding at best. One time, the kitchen fan/light, which was above the table where my husband did a lot of his work, flashed as though it was a Morse code signal. I felt that my husband was trying to communicate with me. I told very few people, but one person whom I opened up to about these odd occurrences suggested that I talk to Chuck and ask him to let me know he was near in a gentler way and in the daytime.

So, I did talk to him, and those nightly occurrences seemed to stop. But one day, I was in my elevator, and as I went down, all the lights went out. Now, here I was in a completely dark, moving elevator; I knew this was Chuck. When I reached the first floor, I told my doorman that the elevator lights had gone out, but when he went to check, they were back on.

I am sure there are doubters who say, "Well, this is all coincidence." But I believe if we're all pure energy when we die, our energy—which never dies—is still able to exist in the atmosphere and affect changes. I had to suspend all prior belief in only the tangible and begin to believe that I could still have a relationship with my husband. I began to feel that if I thought of my husband as *dead*, then he was *dead*.

I was now coming to a realization that Chuck had just made a transition. He passed on from the human plane to the spiritual plane, but we could continue to have a "relationship." I learned that this new relationship would gradually affect my grieving process in a positive way, as I started to create a new life for myself here on earth. Some might call this new relationship with my husband "fantasy." I found it a comfort, and I was able to find answers as I created a life of my own, on my own.

So, how does one person who has lost a spouse continue a relationship with his or her loved one while someone else is not able to? One must be open to new possibilities, to the signs that are all around us. They may or may not come immediately, but they will come if you pay attention. This new relationship or bond can help a person move through the grieving process more easily and more compassionately. When you talk to your loved one, ask him or her for guidance and answers, and I believe that person will come to you as thoughts, ideas, or as dreams as you go about your day-to-day activities.

When I was in my bereavement group, we touched on myriad topics. We became so immersed in each other's stories and lives that it felt like we had known each other all along. The topics we covered were varied. One evening, as we were almost about to close a session, Dan asked, "Does anyone believe in the supernatural?" I raised my hand, as did maybe two or three others. Dan talked to us about having experienced a hug and feeling as if someone was pulling up the blankets over his shoulders as he was about to go to sleep. He then told us when he shared this "crazy" experience with his daughter, she shared that she was having a similar experience.

Dan explained that he felt it was his wife who was coming to tuck him in, and the daughter felt that it was her mother doing the same for her. They both concluded that the mother was attempting to bring them comfort from beyond. I love using the word *supernatural.* It seems to appropriately describe these experiences because it has no religious or spiritual connotation. I believe that anyone can experience making a connection with a deceased loved one, regardless of one's faith background or lack thereof.

I began having a few of these experiences almost immediately: lights flickering, the ceiling fan coming on by itself. Some of these events, when I became fully aware of what was taking place, were actually a bit unnerving, but as I began to share these experiences with a select few people, I found out that my "events" weren't so unusual or isolated. Sometimes these experiences occurred with one or two other people present. Eventually, I began to sense that this was Chuck trying to make his presence known to me and sometimes to others. I began to pay attention so that I could take in the experience and not be afraid.

Another example of a supernatural experience that I had was when my father passed away a few years ago. My father was a very handy guy, and he loved doing things around the house. Many, many, years before—when he first moved into his Manhattan co-op—he decided to lay his own wood floors throughout the apartment. They were beautiful floors that gave the apartment a nice, stylish, finished look. He passed away on a Friday evening in 2005.

The next day, my mother wanted me to take a look at the apartment. She kept saying that something weird was happening to the floors. I went to her home and took a look, and I could not believe what I saw. The floors were beginning to buckle. The parquet tiles had begun loosening and popping up from their foundation. It was the craziest phenomenon. I thought about it and surmised that those floors, which my dad so lovingly laid, were somehow experiencing the sadness of his death and that the energy was so strong it was able to pull the tiles up from the floors. It was as though his beloved home was in mourning, and Dad was letting us know that although he was not in his body, his spirit was still there.

One of the greatest evidences of my husband's presence was on the day that I went back to Sloan-Kettering to be interviewed for my bereavement group. I was actually looking forward to being there, but I didn't anticipate what would occur prior to my acceptance into the group. I caught a cab and relaxed as it traveled down Lexington Avenue in Manhattan (a ride I had taken many times with Chuck). Everything was just fine. I always enjoyed looking at the quaint little shops along Lexington, but as I approached St. Peter's Church, I began to feel a bit anxious.

When I arrived at East Fifty-Second Street, I was feeling full of anxiety. I went into Sloan-Kettering (this was my first time going back there since my husband stopped chemo eight or so months earlier). I passed the very friendly attendant at the concierge desk and rode the elevator up to the office. The woman (who would eventually become part of the two-person team that would facilitate my bereavement group) asked me if this was my first visit back to Sloan-Kettering. I immediately burst into tears.

I had no idea that going back would be so jarring and painful, but it was. I remembered going there with my brother-in-law, sister-in-law, and Chuck early on in 2008 and feeling satisfied and good about our decision to have Chuck treated there. I remembered that dark, rainy evening as we waited with Chuck, all together as a family. I had secretly felt hopeful, but I also knew that our lives would never ever be the same as we began our journey together with my husband.

Now, a year and a half later, all these memories flooded my head, and tears streamed down my face while I told my story to the facilitator. She listened and was so kind and sympathetic. She handed me tissues, I wiped my eyes, and then I left. I felt really drained as I walked out into the street, because I had thought it was going to be a simple interview, and it turned into a sad, traumatic walk down memory lane. It had only been five months since Chuck had passed away, and the wound was as fresh as if it had happened that very day.

On my return home, I caught a cab, and although I noticed it had become quite windy, I really didn't pay attention. As I was riding up Park Avenue, I decided to close my window because it had become a bit cool. I rolled it up and left maybe half an inch of space so that a little air could come into the taxi, then I sat back and a few tears streamed down my face. I was immersed in my sad thoughts when all of a sudden, a pink flower flew into the window—into that little, teeny opening—and landed on my lap.

I was so startled that I let out a little scream. I couldn't believe it, but after a brief moment, I knew that was a sign of comfort from my husband. You see, when Chuck was alive, he brought me flowers all the time. I would sometimes stop in the little shop where he would pick up a few groceries for the house and flowers for me, and the storekeeper would say, "He was just here." So here he was now, trying to let me know that everything was going to be okay. I could almost hear him say, "Sugars, everything is going to be okay. Stop your crying; it's all okay." I took this as a floral note of reassurance. I have the flower today tucked away in a special place.

So, if one is to believe that you can still have a relationship with your spouse, you must suspend all reason and familiar judgment, pay attention, and listen. Faith is believing in that which you cannot see, so I chose to trust that which I could not see and to believe beyond the ordinary.

CHAPTER 7

How Does It Feel to Be Single Again?

One day, as I was standing in the lobby of my building, a neighbor came over to me and said, "You know, I've been thinking about this, and I've been meaning to ask you … how does it feel to be single again?" I was so floored by the question that I couldn't even answer it. To date, it was the most baffling and incredulous, unbelievable question someone had ever posed to me. People can say some really interesting things to one who is grieving, but this question took the cake. I mentioned this to several friends, who were equally as outraged and astonished that someone, would have the audacity and insensitivity to approach me with such a question. I felt like responding, "You were actually thinking about this? Why?"

Many weeks later, however, as I talked with a dear friend of my husband and mentioned this person's inquiry, he suggested that that very question could be a legitimate one for those who had lost a spouse. It made me think of my own circumstance. Once I was a part of a couple, a team, and now I was sadly alone. What did that do to me? How did I feel really, truly? The answer for me was I felt alone. Even though I was surrounded by friends and family, I felt completely and utterly alone.

My husband had been my rock, my compass, my light at the end of the tunnel. He was like a lighthouse, an always guiding and reassuring presence. Now, I was left to create a life that possessed the same sense of security and comfort, but on my own. I decided to take one day at a time. As the days wore on and the days since my husband's passing turned into weeks and months, I found that how I once lived my life with my husband was now evolving into a new way of living without him. Life is like a chapter book. I was beginning a new chapter and probably the most important one of my life. How that would be, what that would look like, I hadn't a clue.

I missed my husband and from the moment of his death, I saw myself as still married to him. As the months wore on, I still continued to wear my wedding band and my engagement ring. I didn't think about dating or future relationships. As far as I was concerned, I still had a husband. He had just died, that's all.

About eight to nine months after my husband had passed away, I kept encountering friends who shared with me their thoughts on my "newly widowed, and therefore, single status." People said things like, "You know, Chuck would want you to go on with your life." Or, "You have so much love in your heart; you'll find someone to be with … a new companion." "You should have someone else to share your life with. It's hard to think about it now, but eventually." "Chuck was such a practical man, and he would not want you to live the rest of your life alone."

All of a sudden, it seemed as if friends were coming out of the woodwork with these bits of advice about my newly single status. However, as far as I was concerned, I was still married to my husband and couldn't bear to think of moving on to someone else. Besides, dating again was a very scary thought. I mean, here I was twenty years later and twenty years older and facing new rules for living and being— and that included dating. There weren't even cell phones back when Chuck and I were dating. Now, there were new rules of engagement. Just the thought of all these new rules and new ways of connecting socially seemed overwhelming and intimidating. Therefore, I decided not to think about it … for a while.

It would be a long time before I began to think about how nice it might be to have a male companion again. Someone to share new experiences with, to laugh with, to talk to, to cry with, to cook with, to have fun with, and someone to just be with. My little life that I was creating for myself was beginning to feel a bit empty. I missed the day-to-day conversations, the lovey-dovey moments, the closeness and comfort of being with a man. I missed having someone to be there for me, and someone I could be there for.

This void really reached its peak when one day I was not feeling well, and as I lay in the bed sneezing and coughing, I wept for the void that Chuck's passing had left. There was no one there to make me soup and tea and to pull the covers up on me. There was no one to rub my face and tell me how sorry he was that I was sick, or kiss my forehead lightly and reassure me that I would be feeling better soon. I then knew that being single again sucked for me.

Now, I know some people might have a different perspective—a new lease on life to be starting life all over again, a clean slate—but for me, I wasn't crazy about being alone, sharing my life with just *me*. But nature has a way of helping us to move beyond our comfort zones. So I decided that eventually, when I was ready, I would seek companionship, a little company, someone to hang out with, talk to, and have fun with, but for now, I knew I was not finished with grieving. I had suddenly reached a point where the tunnel's end had a brighter light, streaming in rays of hope and new possibilities. However, I was still in the tunnel.

Nonetheless, I knew in my heart of hearts, in the depths of my soul, that Chuck was rooting for me. So, soon after the one-year anniversary of my husband's passing, I removed my wedding band and engagement ring and decided to be brave in a new world. And although I wasn't quite sure and was even afraid of what would lie ahead in the future relationship realm, I had reached a point in my grieving journey where I dared to think about the possibility of sharing my life and my love with someone else again.

The thought was daunting. I was afraid that if I got close to someone else again, he could get sick and die. But now I had these crazy thoughts about maybe someday seeking companionship again, and I realized that this was my new truth, uncovered in my grieving journey. I also came to know that I was meant to be a partner, a companion in someone else's life. I'm just wired that way. I knew that Chuck would approve, for I was still here forging a life for myself, with a purpose to fulfill and a destiny to uncover.

For all who are grieving the loss of a spouse, the idea of pursuing a new relationship will either enter your thoughts or not. Oftentimes, the grief-stricken are still in a relationship with the deceased loved one and do not want to end that relationship. Then there are others who cannot bear the thought of going through the pain or grief or possibility of losing another mate. Then still, there are those who start dating soon after their spouse has passed (many times, unconsciously the aggrieved one is trying to duplicate their deceased spouse or replicate the life they sorely miss). And then there are those who feel that they've had their *one*, true love and that was enough for them. However one chooses to proceed, and as the edges of our grief soften, one realization is clear: we have a choice. We can stand frozen in time or move forward with an open heart and the chance to create something new within our lives, which can make one *feel* again.

I remember one session with my acupuncturist, who was treating me for extreme depression. During many sessions I would weep and weep, tears streaming down my face. The grief was so great, but the teary release a relief of grand proportions. After one session I said to my doctor, "Oh, Dr. Lee, I miss my husband so. You know I was married to my soul mate." And he turned to me and whispered in my ear, "There's more than one." And it was at that moment I knew that in this world of so many possibilities, choices, and countless experiences that yes, yes, as far as soul mates go, certainly there must be more than one.

For those who wish to remain solo, really, any choice is okay as long as you're all right with it. Whatever you do, you must dismiss the opinions of others in this matter. You will find that many people around you are so used to seeing you with your spouse that it's hard for them to accept your moving on. Several people have said to me that they felt that I was not ready yet or I was "so lucky to have had the love of my life." One can automatically conclude that that fact precludes you from meeting another "love of your life." But I secretly felt that hope springs eternal, and I began to notice my feelings as I realized that surely God would lead me to the next perfect one for me should I choose to open my eyes and feel with my heart.

CHAPTER 8

The Things That People Say

One of the most difficult things that one encounters when he or she is grieving is the seemingly insensitive things that people say. Most people are well-meaning, but they say some things because they don't know what else to say. Having been on both ends as the condolence giver and the recipient, I know how awkward it can be to find just the right words to say.

Sometimes people don't want to speak about it. They feel uncomfortable with trying to find just the right words. Oftentimes, I noticed that when I mentioned my husband's name to people, there would be a pregnant pause, as if they were awaiting a tidal wave of tears. The topic can become the elephant in the room. People don't want to bring it up, so they'll talk about everything except the deceased loved one. Many times people assume that you are still in the throes of grief, so they avoid bringing it up.

For the most part when my husband passed away, folks were really great. People gave me a reassuring glance or pats or hugs. Most said things like, "I can't imagine" or "I can only imagine how it must feel to lose your life partner, your husband, your best friend." But then there are the occasional statements that some make that leave you wondering if people really think before they speak.

I had a person actually try to equate her separation from her husband to the loss "by death" of mine. "They're both losses," she said. Someone else said, "My husband ran off with another woman, and the only way I can deal with it is by imagining that he's dead, so I can relate to your grief. I feel like I'm a widow too." Huh?

I also received what I will refer to as the "reassuring comparisons"! For example, quite often someone would say something like, "A friend of mine just lost her husband suddenly. She has two small children. She's so devastated and doesn't know what she's going to do. So consider yourself lucky because you had your husband for a long time, your child is grown, and you're in a much better place."

What, as the grief-stricken, am I supposed to do with that? Should I feel ashamed of my own grief? Should I feel better that my circumstance of loss is "better" than hers? Or, maybe I should put everything in perspective by looking at the brighter side of things, which is that we both lost our spouses, but I'm luckier to have spent a longer period of time with mine than my less fortunate counterpart?

When I was faced with these words of "comfort," I would feel anger that somehow now I should be able to get over my grief and that somehow it was not legitimate in the face of others' circumstances. My response would be to not say anything, and I would just withdraw. If people don't really get what you're going through, there is no rule that says you must endure their insensitivity. They think they're being a comfort, but truly they are not.

When someone loses a spouse, it is not a time for comparisons. "My loss is far greater than yours" means very little to a grieving person. You actually risk making the person feel worse, and, as a friend, why would you want to do that? Everyone's loss deserves to stand on its own, and the grieving party should not have to feel that in the case of another's loss, his or her feelings of pain and loss are no longer valid.

The year that my husband was ill was the year that I retired from my profession. A few people actually asked me how I was enjoying my retirement. I chuckle when I think of it now. I would say, "Well, my husband passed away at the same time, so I don't really know." They meant well, wanting to reach out. They wanted to say something, and I guess they felt that was better than asking how I was feeling after my husband had passed away. People didn't want to hurt me or bring up the loss, but they felt the need to say something, just to let me know they cared. All of these people meant well, but some things are better left unsaid. Then there were the crazy things that people said like, "Oh, it's better that he's gone. He suffered so," or "Oh, you'll get over it," or "Oh, you'll get married again as I know how important being married was to you," and on and on.

Sometimes—well, most of the time—I was so surprised with many of the insensitive things that people would bring themselves to say. But as time passed and I put distance between what was said and the person who said it, I realized people were really very uncomfortable with giving verbal condolences. They didn't know what to say. One has to be thoughtful and empathetic in order to know exactly the right thing to say when someone is grieving the loss of a loved one. I decided that I would not hold people to too high a standard as they were just trying to let me know they were sorry without using those words.

I also found it irritating when folks acted as if my husband never existed. Here's one: "Oh, you still haven't gotten over him." Or sometimes people would talk about everything except the person who had died, which, in this case, was my husband. They acted as if he had never existed. However, to deny that this sad event had occurred made me realize that the earth continued to rotate on its axis even though my husband had disappeared off the planet.

I would like to suggest that when people offer condolences, less is more. A mere, "How are you doing?" "I'm here if you ever need me," "I can/can't imagine what you're going through," or, "How's it going?" is enough. I really enjoyed it when people shared a memory. Sometimes someone would tell me something funny that Chuck had done, or they shared some little thing that he had taught them, or they expressed how he had helped them in some way. Hearing someone say, "Oh your husband was so terrific," or "He was a great teacher," or "He was so brilliant; he was such a gentleman," were comforting and welcomed remarks. When someone shared a brief memory with me, it gave me a warm feeling and a connection to the person, and those types of comments were just enough and not over the top.

The other thing I wish to touch on is allowing the grieving person to cry. Thank goodness I am so blessed with such beautiful, loving friends and family. Sometimes I would tell a short story about my late husband or describe a brief moment, and my eyes would well up, and tears fell down my cheeks. It was an inescapable release. My friends would always understand and just sit there or even weep, too. Often we would sit and cry together, and I found those moments to be the most compassionate times spent during my long period of grief. It was a comfort communing with others as they felt my pain.

This is so much better than ignoring the elephant in the room. So it's best not to stop someone who has experienced a loss from that occasional cry. It's best just to be a friend and go with the flow. This is one of those few times where you must step outside of yourself and become truly compassionate. If you admonish the person who is shedding tears to stop crying, or say that he or she is strong, or declare that "there'll be none of that," you run the risk of making a person, who has already experienced the trauma of loss, feel ashamed, embarrassed, or weak. With compassion comes a certain amount of thoughtfulness, mindfulness, and paying attention to the grieving party. It is important that one thinks about what's said so that the aggrieved does not feel judged or admonished. Remember, it's about them, not about you.

One of the many things I loved most about my bereavement group is that with them, I could just be myself in sorrow. If one of us would weep, no one said, "Come on now, stop that crying." Even as I saw myself improving, I still knew that we could talk about our spouses— Ed, Ron, Molly, Connie, Chuck, and Frank—and no one would say, "Don't you think you should be over that by now?" The answer to that question was implicit and simple: No! No! We don't!

CHAPTER 9

How to Remember Those We Have Lost

In the first few days, weeks, and months, I remembered the "perfect Chuck." He was reliable, responsible, beautiful, and perfect. But as the months passed, I began to know that Chuck would not have wanted me to canonize him..He would want me to remember him in the fullness of who he was: an honorable and dignified man who had feet of clay and made his way through this world in the best way he knew how—which was imperfectly. I always contend that if we were perfect, we would not be here on earth. We would have remained in heaven or been born on Venus (you know, the planet of *love*).

In the very beginning, when the loss was so fresh, I was always in my own head. I just remembered the perfect Chuck. My husband really was a superb human being: hardworking, disciplined, generous, and kind; a lover of children and small animals, a great teacher and full of encouragement. He also had a brilliant mind. Chuck knew a lot about most things, and he reminded me of my father in that way. He absorbed information like a sponge.

Chuck took his role as provider and protector of the family very seriously. He was an old-school preppy guy, formal and traditional. Always over prepared for everything, never wanting to be caught off guard by the unexpected, that was my Chuck. My husband was practical, generous with those he loved, steadfast and responsible. He was a motivator and always encouraged others to be their best. He was my idol, and a great example to many who knew him. Recently, I met a friend who said that she had a new principal in the school where she worked. The principal told her that he had taught in the same school that my husband had taught in, and my husband was the reason that he was now a principal. Eventually, when I had a chance to meet this gentleman, he said that Chuck encouraged him and told him that one day he would become a principal. This was part of my husband's legacy: encouraging students and colleagues, family and friends.

Chuck was my hero—the one I imagined in my dream, bounding through fields and leaping over brick walls to meet the fair lady … that would be me. But that was only a part of who he was. He was a pack rat who kept many items from his past like old sweaters from his college days, old correspondence, old T-shirts (even though the logos on some of the shirts were long faded and the old sweaters had holes in them). He also kept many piles of papers, articles, etc. These mile-high piles of clutter caused many Felix/Oscar battles until finally I just said, "I give up." They say a man's home is his castle, so I just allowed half of the castle to remain a mess.

Chuck had gallows humor. This type of humor treats a rather painful matter in an offhanded or lighthearted way. It made me rather uncomfortable when he approached an issue that was highly sensitive and made a joke that was rather inappropriate, but eventually, I adapted to all of this quirky and exceptional behavior. And although I thought I was near perfect, I'm sure he overlooked many of my imperfections as well. We were husband and wife, and that's what you do for the better good of the relationship.

Nonetheless, initially, for many, many months after his death, I remembered the perfect Chuck because he was no longer around in all his humanness. Finally, I realized that he would not have wanted me to retain such a rosy picture of him, giving him saintly qualities. I know he would have preferred that such lofty virtues be preserved for Mother Teresa and the Saints.

When you are grieving, your thoughts about your loved one change and evolve. You will find yourself remembering the good, the bad, and the ugly—and that's okay. After all, it was your spouse's life, and it's best that he or she be remembered—warts and all—every bit whole. Of course, there are those who had spouses who were less than stellar. They may have been crass, rude, nasty, mean, abusive, an alcoholic, etc. I can only imagine that when the person who passed away was not so great, the surviving spouse could feel relieved.

However, these ideas are too simplistic because losses are funny; you could've hated the not-so-great spouse when he or she was alive, and at the same time, still miss that person greatly when he or she is gone. The feelings we have after loss are very complicated, but it's important to take the time to sort them out. I just know that I was caught by surprise when I began to recall the not-so-great Chuck or the gallows-humor Chuck.

After much consideration, I decided that I wanted to remember all of him. He was, after all, a human on this planet. If he was perfect, he wouldn't have existed. So I decided to remember my husband in his totality; otherwise, it would hamper me as I re-created my life and attempted to move on. I soon realized that if the measure of every man after Chuck were to be held to a false "Chuck" standard, then how sad for me. I would be yearning to move on with my life, but I could end up stuck in one place while searching for the elusive.

I tried very hard not to drive myself crazy thinking about the things I could've said, the things I might've wanted to know, the unfinished business, the unknowns. "Why didn't you do that *this* way, Chuck?" or, "Why didn't I ask this question?" Before long, I learned to let the past be the past. There were things I would never know. Surely, according to my own spiritual beliefs, I knew that Chuck now knew everything, and that knowledge tempered my questions and gave me peace, because in the *true* end, those "things" really didn't matter.

CHAPTER 10

Brave in a New World

When I was a little girl, my father encouraged me to be fearless and brave, so I could live my life to the fullest and accomplish my dreams. He did not want me to hinder myself. That was a recurring theme in my life: having courage, being unafraid, and facing the unforeseen. My husband wanted that for me, too, but he also helped me conquer fears and challenges by being there in the background or sometimes, by holding my hand.

When he became ill, my husband became one of the bravest people I have ever known. He rarely complained and wouldn't allow me to ever really know the magnitude of the pain that he was constantly enduring. If I had known, I wouldn't have had the strength or stamina to care for him, to be there for him and pray for a miracle with him, to watch TV with him, to read to him, and just be with him. He had an unbearable existence made bearable by his tenacity, fortitude, strength, belief in God, and will to live—for me.

I believe that Chuck wanted to stay alive for *me*! So he pushed himself to move forward every day. He tried to make his own small meals, do his little errands, go to chemo, and go about the daily routine of living. He remained mentally strong and steadfast, alert and competent, talkative and mobile, till the end. When Chuck passed away, I knew I too had to be brave and go forth in the world, a world that had changed so drastically from my days before Chuck (which I referred to as "BC"). I found that this new world could be overwhelming to me if I allowed it to be.

Initially, after Chuck died, I essentially felt *nothing*; I was going through the motions numbly. And then one day, in midsummer of the year of my husband's passing, I began to feel myself transition slowly from living in a black-and-white world to living in color again. Not high definition, mind you, and no surround sound; just color. It was as if I had been living in the shadow of myself for the past several months, which seemed like an eternity. All of a sudden, I wanted to get back to living. I no longer felt as though I wouldn't survive. Now I wanted to *live*!

My social circle offered me many opportunities to do things and to participate in fun activities: nights out with the girls, exploring the city with friends, lunch, museums, plays with friends, etc. And now that I was retired, I had the luxury of time, so I decided to create a routine for myself that would keep me active, interested, and interesting.

I took yoga classes, went to museums alone, hired a personal trainer, and proceeded to become my best self. Reading and listening to music and meditating and praying—I became hell-bent on reinventing myself. I wanted to stay current so that I wouldn't become a dinosaur. I had met my husband and married in the twentieth century, and now, I was alone in the twenty-first century, where cell phones abound, texting is de rigueur, and I was clueless.

You see, when my husband was alive, we could be clueless together; it didn't matter. We would learn the latest gadgets by and by. I am fortunate that I have a son who inadvertently keeps me current. Albeit, sometimes I'll ask my son the name of a song and he'll tell me, but then add that it was a hit four or five years ago.

So now, with all things celebrity and media driven, I was also creating my next act. I know this sounds like it was all a breeze, but believe me, it wasn't. It took a conscious decision each day to go forth and re-create normalcy in my life. My life after loss had become topsy-turvy. I couldn't believe that such a disastrous event had occurred and that it altered my life as I had known it.

It became important for me to stay organized and on top of things, because there was so much to do. I had a list of tasks for myself and attempted to tackle things sooner rather than later. Initially, I redecorated my home bit by bit, once I decided that staying put in my apartment was going to be the best thing for me to do. I just decided to go for it. I never liked dealing with workmen and always felt relieved when Chuck took care of those tasks. Although I was feeling very vulnerable and alone, now I had become the sole person making decisions, talking with contractors, finalizing projects. I had to do these things bravely and confidently as I "forged a life of my own."

I made changes to my apartment that I knew my husband never would have done nor would he have cared about doing. Chuck thought we had a beautiful home and as long as he had a desk, chair, bed, and refrigerator, everything was copasetic. After he was gone, I needed to re-create my space so that it suited my current lifestyle (whatever that would be), and I needed to smudge the edges of my old life. I would think clearly about whatever project I was undertaking, making swift decisions so as not to get cold feet. Eventually, I found I had moved from the dark, gray days of weeping and great sadness to brighter days filled with hope and courage.

Hope and courage: this was my mantra as I proceeded on that winding road full of faith, hope, and courage and maneuvered around life's twists and turns. When I thought about it, these were the same hallmarks that Chuck and I lived by in our life together and in our marriage. In the beginning, we needed these elements going forward, and we were so full of hope. In the middle of our marriage, we relied on faith in God and our union to pull us through the tough times. And at the end, being brave and having courage helped us both as we moved forward—together and alone—into the unknown.

Someone once said to me when Chuck was in the throes of his illness, "You know, Yvonne, remember that this is Chuck's journey. Yes, the two of you are on a journey together, but this illness is Chuck's journey." Those words gave me a different way of looking at our dilemma. And, remembering those words on the days when I felt myself getting sucked into Chuck's illness, I was able to step outside of Chuck's cancer so that I could continue to be a focused and supportive partner to him, my beloved.

In the months and years after his passing, as I walked this journey alone, I've had to get rid of the old and think about the new. The world as I know it now is very different than the one I knew with Chuck in it, and I've had to adapt. I did it at my own pace, which was, in hindsight, rather swiftly. I began to get rid of those ideas that were limiting and decided to re-create my world so that I would not get swallowed up by the illusions of my mind. I knew that it was important that I try to move forward so as not to become a dinosaur in the twenty-first century. I also know that Chuck would be proud and approve.

CHAPTER 11

The Grief Experience: What One Feels

*I*n her book, *On Death and Dying*, Elizabeth Kubler Ross introduced the five stages of grief that were first applied to those suffering from terminal illness. Later, these were applied to other forms of personal loss, such as the death of a loved one, divorce, and various other incidences of loss and personal tragedy. I found that this model didn't clearly define what the person who was grieving was *feeling internally*, coupled with various physical manifestations. I've identified five stages of the grief journey based on my own personal involvement with the grieving experience.

1. Numbness
2. The Tunnel
3. Teeter-Totter
4. Pinhole of Light
5. Reawakening

The Grief Experience

I will now discuss how I dealt with each experience, step-by-step.

The Five Stages of the Grief Experience

1. Numbness

After Chuck died, I didn't feel his presence. I didn't feel anything or hear anything. I felt completely and utterly alone. I wanted to have a spiritual experience. I wanted to feel something, but I felt absolutely nothing, and the silence was deafening. It was an odd feeling. I felt like, well, maybe he would come back. Then there was the flurry and hubbub of the funeral arrangements, people coming in preparation for the repast, pastoral visits, and everything that accompanies funeral arrangements.

After all the activities died down and everyone left, I felt abysmally sad, afraid, nervous, and numb. My grief was numbing, and I felt so alone in this experience. It was a very intense and painful feeling—like being in a vacuum. I felt as if no one else had experienced anything as debilitating and painful as the emotions and feelings that I was experiencing. The outside world seemed foggy and gray, and I couldn't feel anything; I had lost any sense of joy and happiness. Actually those two emotions had been gone for a while, and now alone, I felt the absence of these feelings in an even bigger way.

It was during this numb stage that my deep, abiding faith began to wane. I felt anger, and I couldn't understand how God had allowed this to happen to me, to Chuck, to us. Chuck had been plucked from my life in an incredibly cruel way. I asked God why he had done this to me, to us. I felt that I had been cheated out of the life that I'd had with my husband, our future together, growing older together, spending the rest of our lives together.

It was during this numb stage that I began to feel that my life at this point was done. Although I didn't contemplate suicide, I do think that if I had walked out into the street and been hit by a bus or had an unforeseen accident, it would have been okay, and I could have been with my husband again. Life for me up until my recent tragedy had been better than most—exceptional really. So what was there left for me to do; remain here and be lonely, missing my husband? My son was a grown man, and he would miss me, but eventually he would be okay, I surmised. My mother and siblings would all go on. But I wasn't sure I could endure the road ahead.

The pain was excruciating, and so to cushion that feeling, I existed in a numb state. I could barely eat; I could barely breathe. I felt nothing but heartache, and I felt very vulnerable and acutely sensitive. No one knew the depths of my despair. No one knew how grief-stricken I was. For many, many months, I existed like a zombie. People would say things like, "Oh, you will be okay. You're so strong; you'll never be at the height of despair." But they didn't know. No one knew that I was nearly beyond that point, and I was in a quandary as to how I could save myself.

2. The Tunnel

There were many days when I felt like I was in some kind of an altered state. It felt like I was in a tunnel with no light at the end. Oh, how I yearned to be able to move forward and see at least a pinhole of light, but that never seemed to occur. I felt suspended in time in a dark, gloomy state, not able to move forward, left, or right. Sometimes I felt off balance; sometimes I felt as though I might lose control. I felt unanchored, no longer attached to the moorings—adrift in a tunnel without a guide.

It was very scary, but after a while, I would find comfort in that tunnel. It was dark in the tunnel; there was no light, no sound, no emotion, just stillness. I was surrounded by my grief, sadness, and depression. I was truly depressed, and that veil of sadness stayed with me in this "tunnel" experience. If I went out on a beautiful sunny day, the bright sun and the hustle and bustle of people going to and fro were a jolt to my being. I could not imagine that people were going back and forth through their daily lives as usual, and my husband had just disappeared from earth. I would soon come to know that that gloomy, dark place was to become a comfort and a retreat where I could weep and meditate and talk to God and Chuck.

Dark and gloomy, sad and lonely, my own little safe place. Life was just too much. There was no light at the end of this tunnel—just a long, dark passageway with no end in sight. This stage occurred simultaneously with my feeling numb.

3. Teeter-Totter

While experiencing the numb state as well as being in the tunnel, I also felt as if I literally would fall off the planet. This, too, was a strange feeling for I felt unsure and anxious—as if I had been let out of a boat and was now floating in water without an anchor. It was an odd feeling at best, scary at worst. On some days, I felt panicky; other days, I felt alone and afraid; and at other times, I felt shaky, afraid to go out, and safer at home.

I didn't feel surefooted, and it was as though if I had one misstep, I could fall apart. I didn't feel secure; I felt as if the bottom had dropped out from under me. Sometimes I thought I might break into teeny tiny fragments, like glass, and become brittle and broken. These feelings of being off balance actually occurred simultaneously with the tunnel feeling. Sometimes I experienced each one by itself, and sometimes I had two or three of these feelings together.

4. Pinhole of Light

My husband passed away in January 2009. As the year progressed, I was still struggling with the first three stages of my grief. Eventually, I was able to begin thinking about my entire life with Chuck and my present life without him. I began to wonder how I would go about creating a life for myself, by myself. I even went through a life review, and I could actually see myself in the present, alone. But surprisingly, one day in early fall of that year, I began to feel slightly hopeful. Soon, I found that I was feeling as though perhaps there could really be a life for me after Chuck's death. This was when I began to see a pinhole of light at the end of the tunnel. It was very tiny, but it was there.

5. Reawakening

By spring of the following year, I began to feel that I had changed. I knew I had to take hold of the reins of my life and move forward. Now, I could actually see myself doing more. Early on, the grief was so heavy that thinking about doing anything seemed like an insurmountable task. Sometimes I was stuck doing nothing. But now, it was 2010. Chuck was still a daily presence on my mind and heart. I still wept daily—cleansing tears, I called them—and all this helped me to grieve as I moved toward re-creating my life.

I began to wonder if I could possibly love again. I felt it was possible, but then there was this fear that if I were to marry again maybe the person would die. I didn't want to go through that again. The thought that I could lose a spouse all over again was frightening, but to love again was really a fleeting thought, which I suppressed as I moved toward the light. Letting go of the grief seemed almost like a betrayal to Chuck in some odd kind of way. I felt if I let go of the grief, I would somehow lose the essence of my husband, or that I wouldn't feel close to him. I would later come to know, however, that I could still be close to Chuck, without clinging to the grief and sorrow.

I was no longer feeling as if I was in the teeter-totter stage. I began to see the colors of life: radiant yellow rays from the sun, clear blue skies, fluffy white clouds, and the blue-white of snow, which caused me to remember how Chuck and I loved to tramp around in fresh, new snow. I no longer dreaded nights or being alone. I was able to enjoy my days from beginning to end and found them filled with myriad rich activities.

I could actually think about how it felt to be retired (since I retired during the time of my husband's illness). I could begin to enjoy not having to be anywhere at any particular time, as well as being able to schedule my life as I pleased. I was revived after a long, long sleep. It happened not suddenly, but unexpectedly over time. Then one day, I was feeling renewed, alive, and reawakened.

CHAPTER 12

How to Grieve

*A*lthough this book is meant to be a guide to grieving the loss of a spouse, this chapter is not meant to be a rigid guideline. It is intended to provide suggestions on how one can get through the sorrow and sadness that accompanies grief. I am sharing my process, hoping it will inform and help those who have lost a spouse or a loved one to get on the road to recovery.

1. **Individual counseling**—I received individual counseling over the phone while my husband was ill. Someone called me from my local Cancer Care organization. Cancer Care, Inc. is a nonprofit organization that provides support services for those who are affected by cancer. There are many other local and national organizations that offer counseling services, and you should go online and find a resource that's right for you.

   After my husband passed away, I received individual counseling at home. This was a great help to me because I was really feeling out of it, but I wanted to move forward in my grieving. To have somebody come to my home, initially, was exactly what I needed at the time. I was very fortunate to have had a person who was very sensitive, kind, thoughtful, and empathetic.

We played soothing music, we talked, I talked and she listened. I cried, and she handed me tissues. We did visualization exercises, and we prayed together at my request once I knew that it was okay with her to pray with me. She also led meditations. I found the individual counseling to be a great preparation and a great help in shoring up my spirit for the next step, which was group counseling.

2. **Group counseling**—Since my husband was treated at Sloan-Kettering Hospital, I was able to go back to them, and they were a great resource for helping me to deal with the aftermath of my husband's death. So back to them I went, and I participated in group counseling when I was ready. Generally, there is a time period between the death of a loved one and when one is deemed ready to be in a group setting.

I reached that mark and was able to participate in the group bereavement sessions. This was an enormous help to me. The fact that all the participants' spouses had been treated for cancer at Sloan-Kettering really helped to bond us in a way that would go deep. We didn't have to explain; we didn't have to paint a picture; we all knew what we had gone through. This was our common thread that moved us forward and has kept us together to this day. They are my grieving family. One of the members, Barbara, coined the name the Journeyettes, and we remain seven people on a journey, survivors.

I would strongly suggest that when someone is grieving, the person should think about joining a group with people who have experienced the passing of a loved one in the same manner.

You wouldn't want to be put in a group where some spouses passed away because of a long illness, while maybe the spouse of another person had been murdered. You wouldn't want to be put into a group where some of the spouses had died suddenly, and your spouse had lingered on with a debilitating illness and then eventually died.

Being in a group where there is a common experience is exactly what you want to look for, otherwise, you may end up having an experience that may not give you the results you want. And what you want is to be able to feel better. You can never bring your loved one back, but at least you can be on the road to feeling better.

In my group, we encouraged each other, praised each other, and most importantly listened to each other as we told our stories over and over and over again. We *never judged* or made one feel that we were taking too long to grieve or that we should move on faster in our grief-stricken state. We respected each other, we respected where everyone was in the grieving process, and we affirmed everyone's right to grieve on his or her own terms. We had each other, and that can mean a world of good to one who feels all alone when he or she loses a husband or a wife. You know that someone is there who has had a similar experience of loss, and you know them. And while it may not bring you comfort, at least you'll know that you are not alone.

3. **Being social**—In the beginning, I just wanted to be alone. I wanted to cry alone, and I didn't want anybody to stop me. I just found comfort in my own thoughts, memories, and grief. Everyone had to respect that. In time, I was able to venture out

and be with friends. After a while, being with friends felt real good.

Not everyone has a network of friends, so my advice is to cultivate friendships, because throughout life, there are highs and lows, and during those lows, you do not want to risk ending up isolated and all alone with no one to turn to, to talk to, or to be with. Even if you have children, they don't always understand or are not able to empathize. Your loss was their father, mother, stepfather, or stepmother, but to you, he or she was your spouse.

Your children's perspective is different. Children, no matter how old, want you to snap out of it and return to being the mom or dad they've always known. They've already lost one parent and they don't want to lose you as well. They may not understand how this tragic event has changed your life, but a friend or a few friends can console you, cry with you, remember with you, hang out with you, and just sit on the phone and listen to you weep—and maybe weep with you. A friend's perspective is different, and even though they're not family, they are probably more understanding because they do not have the same perspective of a family member. They are your friends, and they will be there for you in the best way that they can.

Make sure you seek out those friends who can be there for you in the way that you need. Not all can, and you'd be surprised how longevity in a friendship doesn't necessarily mean that that friend will be the most compassionate toward you. So having a few friends puts you in a position to be able to select who you can bear to be around and who you'd rather not be around in your time of need.

4. **Seeking medical and alternative medical assistance**—I knew early on that I was sinking into the depths of depression. I had never had that experience before, so I knew this was something very different and dark and serious. I felt as if I was free-falling into the depths of an abyss, and I knew somewhere inside of me that if I did not get help, I might not be able to lift myself up out of the very dark place that I was beginning to find myself in.

I went to my physician, and he prescribed an antidepressant. I was not sure if I wanted to go that route, so I also sought advice from an acupuncturist and a homeopathic practitioner. They also prescribed natural and homeopathic remedies to help with my bouts of severe depression. I chose the latter, and I also went to an acupuncturist who claimed that he could treat my depression and possibly help alleviate the grief that I was enduring. This choice worked for me, and over time, I did begin to feel better about my life and my loss. It was a slow process, although I must say it was quicker than I expected, and gradually I found myself feeling better.

So I would suggest that as you begin to feel yourself sinking deeper and deeper into grief, it would be a good idea that you consult with your choice of a physician or an alternative holistic practitioner. The alternative route may not work for everyone as well as it did for me. But whether you consult with a traditional doctor or choose an alternative health practitioner, know that they will be a great help in guiding you in your search for ways to feel better so that you can function day to day.

5. **Exercise**—Many months after my husband's passing, I developed an exercise routine, and I even hired a personal trainer. I wanted to create some healthy practices for myself

so I thought I would start with exercise, yoga, weight training, and other physical activities. This was really great, and the new routine helped to improve my outlook toward my future as I began to improve the way that I looked and felt. I also found that as the endorphins kicked in, I began to feel more alive and more a part of life.

The yoga helped me to focus and to concentrate, and it helped give my mind a break from thinking about the sad things. Yoga gave me the discipline I needed to begin to channel my energy into other areas of my life. This routine helped me to become active. I felt empowered, stronger, and less afraid, and I began to feel like I was now again a part of the living.

So, I would suggest that those who are grieving find ways to get out there and get moving at your own pace. Walking is a simple way of getting fresh air, exercise, and a fresh outlook on your circumstance. You will feel more alive, and you will feel as though you are doing something for yourself. As you concentrate and focus on self-improvement, your mind will feel more rested. You'll begin to feel encouraged, and one day, you might even find yourself laughing, smiling, and beginning to enjoy the sight and scent of flowers, the beauty of the sky, or the sound of a child's laughter. Your steps as you walk will become livelier. All this will happen subtly, but it will happen as you begin to step into your new life with both feet.

6. **Silence**—This aspect of my grieving was probably the most important part of the process. Finding time to be silent meant not answering the phone, not sending an e-mail, and not answering the doorbell. I selected a period of time during each

day to get quiet, be one with myself, be one with Chuck's spirit, and be one with God.

It was during this time of the day—usually in the morning—before any thoughts or the noise of the day entered my spirit, I would collect my meditations, Psalms, and prayers, and I would just be one with God and myself. This was a time when I was able to talk to Chuck as if he were right there with me. I would ask him questions, and I would ask God many, many questions—and I would weep and weep and weep.

Sometimes I would just think about the things that Chuck and I had experienced together. I would think about my life and how I was going to make it without my husband. This also became a time when I would plan in my mind or imagine the things that I might do going forward. Whatever I thought during these periods of silence, they were my own thoughts, and they were the thoughts that inspired me, lifted me, and helped move me forward.

Everyone needs a period of silence every day. I do not mean that you should estrange yourself from others, but it should be more like a self-imposed quiet time so that you can be one with your thoughts and your most cherished friend ... you! During this time, set goals for yourself (that you keep to yourself), and then continue to keep your eyes on the target that no one else sees.

No one has to know what you're thinking or planning for your life. You do not have to be exposed to anyone else's judgments, criticisms, or opinions. You are dedicating time to yourself. You are your greatest consultant, because only you know yourself best. You will find that being silent helps you to renew your spirit and moves you toward a life that is meaningful, less sorrowful, and filled with love for yourself.

CHAPTER 13

My Husband—Clarence Cortez Loftin, III

This part of the book is the most difficult to write, but I can't imagine writing this book without devoting a chapter to the very person who inspired it. My experience with grieving his loss is what moved me to put pen to paper.

My husband's name was Clarence Cortez Loftin, III, but he was "Chuck" to all who knew him. He was a truly magnificent human being who taught and inspired many with his good example, business and financial acumen, incredible teaching skills, and the counsel he gave to others.

One of the things about the death of a loved one is that once the person has passed away, one may only remember the person in the best light. We have a tendency to re-create the person in the best way, forgetting the totality of the person, the way he or she really was. Chuck was not a superhuman, but he was, like all of us, determined to live life to the best of his ability—not perfectly, just the best that he could. He was a man who had a no-nonsense demeanor. He was not the kind of guy you called up and said, "Let's grab a couple of beers."

Chuck was serious, cerebral, logical, rational, and fixed. He cared about others, but was not one to go out of his way to assist. He was someone who would help, and he always hoped that the assistance he gave would be enduring. We had many fun times, as did he and his family, but he was not a fun guy. He had a gallows, dry humor, which could be rather off-putting until you got to know him and knew that this style of humor was just a part of who he was.

Chuck started out with an MBA and a career in business. He became a vice president at the Equitable Life Assurance Corporation (Equico Capital Corporation), and he worked as a venture capitalist, assisting in financing many minority-owned small businesses, some of which still exist today. Chuck played a major part in the early stages of the growth of *Essence* magazine. He worked with such notable businessmen as Earl Graves, Travers Bell, and Reginald Lewis, and he had a great commitment to the growth of African-American–owned businesses. As an undergrad at Howard University, he and his best friend started a business model that was so unique at the time, it received accolades from the mayor of Washington, DC. Later in his career, Chuck served as the general manager of the *New York Amsterdam News*, a well-known New York City African-American newspaper. He was tenacious, brilliant, hardworking, and proud.

Chuck loved to teach or impart information to others. He eventually became an adjunct professor in finance at several local colleges. Later on in his career, Chuck also became a teacher for the New York City Department of Education where his enthusiasm for teaching, his hands-on approach, and his ability to get children excited about science, math, and social studies helped him to become one of the most sought-after teachers in the district. He was black, he was male, and he was a good role model for all young people. He became one of the most well-loved and well-respected teachers in his school.

As I recently looked over some of the notes and cards that the children sent to him while he was ill, they're full of thank-yous for "being the best teacher," or "for giving them the best experiences," or for helping them to expand their worldview. One particularly moving note was from one of his colleagues who shared how when she passed Mr. Loftin's science room, which was now dark and vacant, she always felt so sad.

Chuck was generous, loving, caring, and beneath the tough exterior a very sensitive and compassionate man. He rarely showed that side of himself. He was rather conservative, although not in his politics. In his handling of finances, situations, and people, he used temperance before he reacted. He was never quick to react or respond, but always prepared for anything. Chuck was the type of guy who had twenty flashlights, ten pairs of scissors, and fifty screwdrivers, just so that if there was ever a need, he would be prepared (even if it meant being overly prepared).

He never wanted to be caught by surprise in any situation, thus Chuck always had his guard up. My husband was a type A personality, although to the outside world, this was not initially apparent. He seemed like a very smart but laid-back guy. He was also a grudge holder, although he said that he was not. He just felt that he should keep his friends close—although not too close—and his enemies far, far away.

Chuck was no-nonsense and very practical. He was also a very loving husband and father. He was very generous with my son (his stepson) Karim and me. Chuck bought me flowers almost on a weekly basis, and little blue boxes from that famous Fifth Avenue store were frequent expressions of his love for me and appreciation for all I represented to him. It was fitting that after Chuck had passed away, I received an e-mail from a dear friend of his that simply stated, "I will miss his counsel." This was typical of the many notes and e-mails and phone calls I received from many of his friends and buddies.

Chuck was very competitive—sometimes even to a point where he might lose a friend or two—but I always waited until I felt he would be receptive and tried to tell him that he may have overreacted to a particular situation. That was probably his Achilles' heel, the fact that he did not like to be criticized; he didn't like to be advised, no matter how old the advisor was. They could be one hundred years old; Chuck did not like to be told what to do. Nor did he like to be made to feel that something he had said was incorrect.

You know the world moves on whether you like it or not. It doesn't wait for you to catch up emotionally, psychologically, technologically, etc. So Chuck suffered from not being able to change with the times, still holding on to old ways, grudges, and antiquated ideas. He had a hard time stepping into the present day because part of him was still back on "The Street," as Wall Street was referred to, and he had a hard time acknowledging that there were newer guys on the street with fresher ideas that superseded old ways.

That was my Chuck: not perfect, but a man who was complex, yet simple and loving. He was my curmudgeon. He was so bright, dignified, classy, and cultured. He knew everything and if he didn't, he made *you* search for the answers. His approach was to empower everyone he met.

As a husband, he was truly my protector, provider, and teacher. He was always there, in the best of times and in the worst. He was always full of good, sound advice.

When pancreatic cancer was formally diagnosed, Chuck chose to deal with it in a way that would keep me encouraged. He created a journal of empowering and healing thoughts and ideas, webs and maps, drawings and pictures. Some days he felt like he would "beat this thing," and others he asked God, "Why do I feel like this is a losing battle?"

My husband was a very dignified man. One of our last outings was when we walked into New York's Central Park one day and continued over to the tennis courts. We sat down on a bench opposite the tennis courts, and my husband proceeded to lie down on the bench. Now, this was an act that Chuck would never have done ordinarily, but I know he just had a sense of abandonment and despair—and a feeling that it didn't really matter anymore.

As he lay on the bench, he looked up at the sky, and I knew that he was communing with God. I knew that he was trying to figure out how it was going to be up in the sky, in heaven. He was in his own thoughts, and I sat by him pretending to read a book, but quietly weeping. We slowly walked out of the park, and we stopped at the ice cream man on Central Park West. My husband loved sweets, and he loved ice cream. We purchased a couple of pops, and we brought them upstairs.

Now in the old days, Chuck would've been able to eat both pops in one sitting, but now he took a bite and put both in the freezer. He ate a little off of the pops every day until they were gone, and that must have taken at least two weeks. We never went back to the park again, and it would be a long time before I would be able to step foot in Central Park. In time, I would, but it would be with great effort.

My husband always maintained his dignity to a point where I was never really sure how much pain he was in until a few months before his passing. We had gone to the emergency room, and when we arrived at the hospital, the intake nurse asked him what his pain threshold level was on a scale of one to ten. He answered "eight." It was then that I realized how he had been suffering in silence. I couldn't imagine the excruciating pain he had been experiencing. All along he had been suffering in silence, maintaining his dignity till the end.

Soon after my husband passed away, it was hard for me to remember him before his illness. I could only remember Chuck as he was when he was ill. That period when Chuck was ill became the ever-present picture in my mind whenever I thought of him, dreamed of him. My mind seemed to block out the previous Chuck: robust, healthy, vibrant, and alive. Even when I dream about Chuck, which is very rare (maybe six dreams since he passed away over five years ago), he was always in that state of illness—frail, thin, and weak. Over time, I found that I was able to picture Chuck as he really was when he was healthy. When I was able, which was not for quite a few years, it helped to look at pictures in order to recall my husband in the fullness of who he was for most of his life.

Even now as I think of him, I know that I want to honor him as a whole person. I don't want to hold on to a faulty illusion. In the beginning, after his death, I could only remember the idealized Chuck, but in time, I remembered the foibles, the weaknesses, the lows, the fullness and entirety of all that was my husband, Chuck Loftin. I know that he wouldn't want me to canonize him. I imagine that he now understands his earthly life more fully than he ever could have while still here. He was human, after all. He possessed flaws as well do I. But in his entirety, he was the best of the best, and I loved all of who he was. He could only be the way he was, and who he was is what carried him on his journey in his life here on earth.

I have allowed myself to evolve into who I am now without his physical presence, but I still feel his love and assurance. I imagine that he is rooting for me to carry on and to create the best life that I possibly can without him. I imagine that he would want me to continue my life in its fullest, wishing for it to be fruitful, joyful, creative, rewarding, and full of fun.

My husband, Chuck, was honorable, forthright, dignified, and my soul mate. But as I have continued on this journey, I have been able to glimpse the endless possibilities for my life, and I now believe that with regard to soul mates, there are more than one. I also know that Chuck would approve.

CHAPTER 14

Others' Thoughts on Grieving

*M*ost of us at some point in our lives will be confronted with the loss of a loved one. Everyone has his or her own way of dealing with the death of a loved one. I was curious as to how other people felt and dealt with losing someone very close to them. This chapter includes thoughts by others about their own experience with grief and loss. I share these words, hoping that someone else's experience, which may be different than mine, will resonate with the reader. Hopefully, as you go through the grieving process, you will not feel so alone.

Roberta G.: My husband died from cancer in 2008. In the beginning, my feelings were of disbelief and grief. It is now 2012, and although I am not at the end of my grieving journey, I am definitely further on in that journey. In the beginning, it was foggy, but I was not able to stay there because of the responsibilities I now had of raising my son alone. I moved back to my hometown, and after an adjustment, I found that I eventually had a real sense of loneliness.

I would suggest that one grieve honestly. I still talk to my husband and always know what he would say. When I had my first dream of my husband after his death, I awakened with a confused feeling, not knowing if I should feel pain. I decided that I was happy because I had not expected to make any new memories with my husband, and the dream was exactly that. I believe that when one begins the grieving process, it is totally an individual process. Even though society does expect one to move on, I do not believe that there is a time limit on grief. When those who are grieving find themselves in enormous pain, I strongly suggest that they search for a support group or get help through counseling.

There are so many changes that one goes through as one grieves. I think that the Kubler Ross model is very real, but each person goes through the stages differently. For me, the death of my husband gave me strength or perhaps a new perspective on making choices and feeling strong about them. If something hurts too much, then I know it's okay to let go. If something feels right, even if it seems sentimental or for some, wallowing, then I say it's okay.

When it comes to timetables, when one is dealing with a loss, you have to ignore them as best as you can. I think people who really care only put you on a timetable in hopes that you can move forward and perhaps find peace or happiness. I also knew that if I remained in the tunnel too long, I might permanently dwell there. I would add that my husband would be mad at me if I didn't get my act together.

When I think about faith as an assist with grieving, I believe that faith is elusive, but for me, if I didn't have faith, then I wouldn't know where my husband is now. I asked him once, in my mind, if heaven was all we hoped it would be, and he replied, "It's better." That gave me more comfort than anything else. When I think about the unanswered questions, the unresolved hurts, the unfinished business, the things we would like to have known but were never able to get answers for, I believe that although we can no longer get those answers in death, the questions don't matter so much. In the end, I believe that being brave honors the ones we've lost.

Rev. Dr. Arnold Isidore Thomas: I lost my brother, Lee, to AIDS when he was thirty-two years old back in 1984 (I was thirty). My father died in 1990 at the age of eighty-six, and my mother died in 2008 at eighty-seven. While my parents' deaths had an enormous impact on my life, it was my brother's death that affected me most.

I had prepared for his death for a while since AIDS back then was the diagnosis of certain death. Yet despite the inevitability of his death, when I heard the news of his passing, an important piece of my life that was defined and identified in relation to him died with him. I had lost my brother and closest friend, the one whose history was most intertwined with mine; the one with whom I wanted to grow old and reminisce about the past; the one whom I asked to be the godfather of my first child and who I knew would be the favorite uncle of my children.

All of that was suddenly gone in the moment of his death, and I felt so empty and alone. It took me a couple of months to adjust to the fact that he was gone. These months included intentional days of solitude from church and family to deal with the stark, cold reality of his absence. They included dreams of his presence that seemed so real I didn't want to wake up; but I had to wake up to the fact that I had a wife and child on the way who needed me. I also had a letter from Lee to his godson whom he would never meet in the flesh, blessing and encouraging him with instructions and guidance he had hoped to give him in person. I needed to make sure that I at least lived long enough for him to read and understand it, and to share the life of my amazing brother.

In the beginning, I had always believed in an afterlife and knew that God had not caused his suffering. I believe that whatever happened, God would always be with Lee. But I wanted Lee to be with me as well; so I prayed that God would grant me a miracle, even selfishly hoping the Almighty would cut me some slack since I was one of God's clerics. Lee died the morning of Good Friday—what timing! So the narrative of Christ's passion was one that my brother and I were walking together "through the valley of the shadow of death" (Psalm 23:4).

When I think about how I got from "there" to "here," "there" was the Holy Week from hell. When Lee died, my prayer to God was the same prayer Christ uttered from the cross: "Why have you forsaken me?"(Psalm 22) After all, I had cared for and consoled countless individuals and families who had suffered enormous loss. As their pastor, I should exemplify faith and fortitude in times of tragedy. They needed a faith leader who would not be blown away by storms of despair. I felt that I was failing the "times of trial test," and questioned whether I was fit to continue on in ministry. That was what "there" was like.

The "here" was always in battle with the "there," reminding me that loved ones, including my wife and soon-to-be-born child needed me. I had to get through this. I had to get over "there." In many ways, the Holy Week vigil of walking with Jesus through his passion and resurrection was therapeutic. It was as if God was saying, "No one, not even Christ, is spared the inevitability of emotional and physical suffering, or death. They are attributes of life, and the experience of pain and loss becomes the tie that binds you in fellowship and empathy with the rest of humanity."

I could now more fully grasp the sorrow another encountered in the death of a loved one having suffered such loss myself. But having suffered such loss, I could once again rejoin the network that supported and saved me from falling too deeply into the abyss of despair; a network of faith that assured me in the dawning light of Easter that the grave has no victory and death has no sting.

As earlier mentioned, it took a couple of months to get fully from "there" (the beginning of my grieving journey) to "here" (the present), and it was a hard journey; but a journey I was able to see through because of faith in God's eternity that lives in Lee and us all.

I would suggest that one grieve honestly. Provide yourself the needed time to be in silent solitude, to cry and scream and howl your feelings to God, to honestly deal with the loss of someone precious to you. Don't feel constrained to conform to someone else's agenda or time frame for grieving. However, be aware and sensitive to the fact that you, too, are also loved and needed, and while you are grieving, others will be concerned and praying for you.

If you are a spouse or parent, realize that members of your family continue to rely on you and are hoping that your grief, while warranted, will not overshadow their love and need for you. Realize also that if your loss was as great a personal loss for them, they too will need to be consoled and supported and to be assured that you are not so consumed in grief that you are unable to notice theirs.

So, by all means, recognize your emotional needs in times of grief, but never in isolation from others you love. Share your thoughts and feelings with them, acknowledging both your needs and theirs in getting through this time of mourning and respecting the need for both solitude and community and for both self-healing and (possibly) personal and or/group therapy. The objective of grieving in this way is to heal rather than to sink deeper into depression. And to this end, it is vital to know that in times of great loss, while you may now and then need to be alone, you are also an integral part of a caring community that will never abandon you.

Ann J.: In 1994, my mother died suddenly. Five months later, my father died. I lost both parents in the same year. It was a real shock to my whole body. However, the greatest loss was my husband, of only eight years, who died suddenly Thanksgiving weekend in 1999. After my mom died, I was numb but on autopilot because there was so much to do. After my husband, Thom, died, I felt as if I had six hundred tons of bricks on my chest. I felt lost and alone. It took four years of grief counseling and therapy and using the skills I've learned to continue healing in order to get "here" where I am today. Being "there" was trying to find out where I fit, what I was going to do with myself, and finding out what God wanted of me. "Here" is being in the light as opposed to being in the dark.

I would suggest that one grieve in whatever way allows that person to heal. In my experience, the grieving process began right after I took care of the immediate necessary business. So for me, it was sooner rather than later. For me, the gain was discovering that I had a new life to live but with the memory of the wonderful life that I no longer had. In my opinion, there is no limit on how long one should mourn as long as grieving doesn't become the reason for one's existence.

I did not allow anyone else's timetable to influence the length of my grieving process. It takes as long as it takes. My grief counselor made that very clear. One must believe that there is a light at the end of the tunnel and, with help, one must continue to look for it. My belief in God was the only way I got through the loss of my husband. It was the belief that God was walking with me through the process. As for the unfinished business: unfinished business remains unfinished, unanswered questions remain unanswered. I think we leave this earthly journey with lots of unfinished business and unanswered questions. It's part of the human condition. My trust in God helped me to accept that. I also believe that one remains brave with the help of supportive friends and family and with God's help.

Bonnie Cehovet: I lost my father just before I turned thirteen years old, nearly fifty years ago. Initially, I experienced disbelief that this had happened, anger at God, emotional pain so severe that it made me physically ill. It has taken me fifty years to get from "there" to "here." "There" was a very difficult place. I could not talk about my father's passing with my mother because she was so devastated. She sent me to talk to my father's physician, who was a cancer specialist and had little rapport with a child who had lost a parent.

Even after all this time, I have not completely healed, but I have healed to the extent that I can. I no longer blame God, and I believe and understand that we can choose to leave the physical world at any time if our work is finished. I believe that my father went on to do other work and learn other lessons on another plane.

I would suggest that when one is grieving, you must allow yourself to cry, to rant, and to rail; whatever you need to do. Recognize that grieving is a process, and we all go through it differently. Trust plays a huge part in grieving. We have to trust that the crossing over happened in its own time, which was the right time for the individual involved. We need to trust that we can reconcile any differences that we might have had with that person while they were still in physical form. We need to trust that our prayers will be answered. We need to trust that a better time will come and that we will heal. I believe it is possible that you can continue a relationship with someone who has passed on. You can connect with them in dream time, you can write them letters, and you can talk out loud to them.

Trust that the responses you see/hear/feel are from them. I don't really think that we choose when the grieving process begins. I believe that if there has been an extended illness, and death is expected, that grieving starts before the death. In other instances, the grieving starts as soon as we are notified that there has been a death. Grieving begins on an internal level, one that we might not become aware of until it manifests in our consciousness. When there is a loss, one gains perspective—perspective on what was, what is, and what will be. But I think it's important for those who are grieving to embrace the pain and not attempt to deny it. At first, it will be overwhelming, but we do work our way through to the other side, to a bearable level.

There is no time limit on how long one should grieve. Grief takes us as long as it takes. However, one does not want to become stuck at any given level in the grieving process. If you recognize that this is what is happening, then seek outside help. Grief counseling or therapy might be an answer for you.

Pain and suffering over the loss of loved ones is, to me, an acknowledgment of how much they meant to me; of the important part those people played in my life. The experience can be lengthy, and it can be surreal. The changes that I experienced along the many years of my grief over my father made me a stronger, more spiritual person. The experience helped me to find myself. It takes time to find a new balance in your life.

Some rituals we will hold on to because they bring us a sense of peace and security. Some rituals we will need to let go of. Only when we have released the painful rituals can we replace them with something that brings us peace. Those who have experienced loss need to be strong enough to stand up for themselves. No one is experiencing their grief but the person himself. No one can, in good conscience, put limits on someone else's grief.

Eventually, I was able to see the light at the end of the tunnel, and one of the ways I did that was through prayer. At first, I railed at God through my prayers, but I eventually made peace with him. The light at the end of the tunnel was, for me, spiritual acceptance of my loss. For those of us who believe in God, we must know that we do not walk alone, and knowing that makes all the difference in the world. Speaking to your loved ones through prayer or taking them into dream time with you will help you to answer some of those unanswered questions. Be willing to listen and hear those answers.

We remain brave in a new world when we recognize that we indeed live in two worlds—our private world, and the face that we show the public. Eventually the worlds begin to overlap, and we start to experience healing.

Vince Hill: My wife, Janis, passed away in January, 2011, of complications from breast cancer. She was a former NFL cheerleader, but that wasn't her claim to fame. She often said she "loved being Vince Hill's wife and the mother of his two sons." She was my best friend and the love of my life. I was truly blessed in having found her.

Grieving is something that is very personal and private and I am not the person who should decide when, how long, and how a person should handle any kind of loss, whether it's expected or unexpected. Everyone handles the loss of a loved one differently. The textbooks will tell you that there are five (sometimes seven) stages of grief: denial and isolation, anger, bargaining, depression, and acceptance. What you're not told is the stages come in no particular order and, sometimes, the stages are very much delayed.

When I *accepted* my wife's passing in the waiting room of the hospital, I lost any sense of reality. One of the first things I said to myself was, "I'd better call Mom and Dad," but that was impossible since they had passed years before. *Denial* had immediately set in.

The people who "came to my aid" during this ordeal were the people I grew up with—some I hadn't seen or heard from in nearly forty years. I eventually asked one friend, who I knew was a widow, "When does it stop hurting?" Her response was, "It happened twenty years ago, and I have since married a wonderful man. It hasn't stopped hurting." Or, a woman I work with, who told me about the death of her husband while holding back the tears: "It never stops hurting." She has since remarried as well.

Some men have extramarital affairs before and love affairs after their wife's passing. They handle their grieving quite differently than I did, but I'm not the one to judge. When my wife had a double mastectomy, I took a vow of celibacy (*isolation*). Even though I still saw the woman I met over thirty years ago as beautiful, she said she felt ugly, no longer having breasts and no hair. I promised her we would have no intimacy until she was cancer free and well. She gained weight because of the cancer drugs and felt very insecure. I then gained weight and promised her we would go on diets together once her danger had passed. She was comfortable with this.

People who have lost loved ones will say, "She's in a better place." My response, to their shock, is, "Her better place was waking up in bed next to me every morning and being healthy." Yes, I have said this to a few pastors (the *anger* phase).

When I think about bargaining with God, I ask myself, "What? Am I going to make a deal with God, and she'll come back to life?" Once, I actually did say to myself when I went to pick up her belongings from the hospital, that maybe if I ask real nicely, the doctors can bring her back to me.

You know it's time to start finding a new partner in your life when your late wife's girlfriends start introducing you to women *they* think will be good for you. This is not a good idea in any way, shape, or form. But that will be the subject of *my* book.

David J. Esq.: I lost my son in 2000 to gun violence. It came as quite an unexpected shock. It has been fourteen years, and I still have not been able to put it into my rational perspective as to why it happened.

My feelings right after this experience were utter shock that literally knocked me to the ground. After the shock, I would say that the next reaction was disbelief. The most intense period of my grieving lasted about two years. After that, the pain gradually subsided, but I think that I will always live with the loss as a residual sadness in my life.

When I think about what the "there" was like for me, I remember that my initial feeling was total shock, and then immediately it turned to disbelief. For years I did not believe that I had actually lost my son, even though it was a fact. To a degree, the feeling that subsists is my belief that he lives on somehow and somewhere. This thought is more on the level of a religious or spiritual belief, the sense or an intimation that something else is out there.

During the two years of intense grieving, I accepted the fact that I had indeed lost my son, but during that period of time, it was not something that I could discuss without breaking down and crying. My emotions were all out of whack, and I became somewhat reclusive.

Indeed, Christmas, a holiday that I love, was and still is, to a certain degree, difficult to get through because I remember how much my son loved Christmas and how we approached it as true believers up to his death. Imagine, an eighteen-year-old kid not wanting to get out of bed too early on Christmas for fear of seeing something he wasn't supposed to see (a bearded man with toys?).

That's the kind of up and down that you feel with grief. Happiness can become sadness and vice versa. During this period of time, I was wearing more of my grief on my sleeve than I realized. Total strangers would say to me that I looked like I was angry and wanted to fight. This, of course, was far from the truth. I just wanted no part of the world during this time. I guess that people who didn't know me and some of my friends interpreted this manifestation of grief as anger.

The "here" is simply a resignation to the loss with the residual sadness that I will have for the rest of my life. It gets more tolerable every day now, and I can talk about my son without crying.

I would not give any suggestions to anyone on how to grieve. It is a personal experience, and one has to work it out in any way that one can. I may also note that I have only talked about the loss of my son here, because that is the loss that shocked me the most. But I also lost my parents and my best friend, and I had to grieve those losses, as well as the loss of my favorite pet. I think we have different ways of grieving different losses. Losing my parents was also hard, but I expected that it would come at some point, and they had had full lives. With losing my son, however, I had to reconstruct myself because it was such a shock and such a loss.

On some level, trust is important. You have to turn to a higher being and realize that one will get through the process and hopefully end up being whole again at the end of it.

When it comes to the question of wondering whether it's possible that you can continue a relationship with one who has passed on, my answer is one of a spiritual response. I think that initially, it is important to realize that the person still lives on in some fashion, but eventually you will come to the true realization that the person has passed on. Sure, my son is still alive in some way, but he is in another dimension that I cannot really reach in this life. I have to continue living the best that I can so that I can move on when it is my time.

When I think of the grieving process and the question of when it begins, I feel that one does not have a choice when one is going to begin the grieving process. It starts with the loss, and one does not have control over that.

As I think about what one gains after a loss, I don't necessarily like to think of it as a gain, but one does have to re-create oneself after a great loss, and you gain insight into yourself and into God. Each person has a different way of dealing with loss, and I cannot suggest a way of dealing with the pain except to say that you have to find your inner self and your spiritual self to deal with loss.

When it comes to a time frame for grieving, I feel that there is no limit on how long one should grieve. It is probably a lifelong process. I still think of life in terms of before losing my son and after losing my son. But, I would say that the very difficult period of grieving probably lasts anywhere from one to three years. For me, I cried every day for two years and had very little relief from my grief. As I said, I could not even talk about my son without crying. After those two years, I still felt the loss, but I was able to discuss it. I doubt very seriously that I could've talked about grief or loss or anything like I am now during that initial two-year period of time. You have to go through the process to obtain better insight and to get through the pain. In time, one obtains better insight into oneself and gains a better spiritual understanding.

When it comes to the question of finding a new balance, as I began to transition my life without my son, I found myself continuing to cherish the things that we used to do together. My son and I used to run together, and I always enjoyed that even when I couldn't keep up with him any longer. To this day, it may be a reason that I continue with physical fitness. I always see him a little bit ahead of me, and in my mind's eye, he probably is still running with me. As for the timetables that other people put on one's grieving, I would not accept any timetables that anyone else puts on me. They don't know, they are not there, so how can anyone put a timetable on you? At a certain point, you really have to tell people that they can go somewhere else.

As for the light at the end of the tunnel, the pain gets easier to deal with as time goes on. I'd say one to three years is the period of intense grieving; after that, it becomes livable. I would occasionally look at movies about grieving. There was one with Nicole Kidman called *Rabbit Hole*, which I liked. The premise was that there are many different levels of existence and that we may all live in different realities simultaneously. She had also lost her son in this movie, so she said to the person who told her about the rabbit hole, "Oh, you mean that in some other life, I am actually happy? What a refreshing thought." The character in that particular movie had also been in a group therapy session, and eventually she left it because she thought that what the other people were doing was stupid.

This gets me back to my original premise that grief is a personal thing, and what works for some people will not work for others. Although most people will confront their spiritual selves during the process of grieving, others may turn their backs on their religion during the process. It's different for everyone. But to get back to the main question, the light at the end of the tunnel will eventually manifest itself. It is personal, and it is different for everyone. One day, the intense period of grieving will be over, but you will not know it until after it has passed, and you are able to assess where you are.

If one has faith, it will help you in your grieving, knowing that your loved one has passed on to an eternal life. However, for one to think that just because you have strong religious beliefs that you are not going to feel the pain of loss would be incorrect. I think that religion will help those who have strong religious beliefs, but it is not going to save you from the grief. Indeed, at some point you have to get beyond religious beliefs and confront the fact that although your loved one will have eternal life, he has still left this world and is dead. As for the unfinished business, the unresolved hurts, the unanswered questions, everyone has this as well as self-doubts. You just have to accept the fact that there are things that were not said that could have been.

In this new world that you now inhabit without your loved one, you will remain brave, but don't be afraid to cry. It helps you to move on. This may be another one of those questions that is hard to explain because, really, why do you have to be brave? Why is that even necessary? People used to tell me that I was being very brave. That made no sense to me because I was crying every single day for two years. I couldn't admit that to anyone because as a man, one is not supposed to cry. So, I guess I was not being brave because I was crying, and when I admitted that to people, they thought that I was taking things too hard. But, hey, that helped me get through the experience. So, I am not sure whether it made any difference whether I was brave or not. Who cares? The main thing is that I got up every day during that two-year period of time, went to work, and otherwise got through the day.

The question of being brave kind of reminds me of a situation where one is thrown into the sea, a mile or two away from land, and now you're forced to swim to shore even though you never swam more than a few yards in your life. When you get to shore, someone says you were brave because you made it to shore. You look at them incredulously and say, "Brave? I didn't have a choice. I didn't swim because I was brave but because I had to stay alive." It seems like that's the same way with grieving; one doesn't grieve bravely, one grieves because one does not have a choice.

The truth of the matter is that for a long time, I tried to escape from my emotions and did not begin to really effectively mourn until I confronted them.

When I think about the light at the end of the tunnel, although I think I have gotten past that stage, I have to continue to realize daily that I'm still alive and that it is important to confront and cherish the world every day.

Robin B.: My husband died unexpectedly. This occurred hours after a dear friend, whose funeral I was in the midst of planning, had died. When my husband passed away, I experienced pain, sadness, deep grief, and numbness. These feelings were all further compounded by the reality that our only child, a sixteen-year-old high school junior, had lost her dad.

The grieving journey for me has been a never-ending journey. After the first six months, my journey to get to where I am now began. Each day gets better, but certain memories bring it (grief) back. I began to manage my new normal as I worked to move on with my life journey. I had to also always be there for our daughter, and she did the same for me. Bereavement is such a personal journey, and one should choose to grieve any way they want to when they're ready.

I have continued to have a relationship with my husband through prayer, memories, and conversation with others. When it comes to dealing with the pain of loss, I'm not in a position to begin to make a suggestion. Each person's pain is individual and can be very different from mine. We all handle pain differently; some may need to face it head on, and others may need medical/professional assistance.

I found my journey through grief to be a cathartic experience. I found that as I transitioned into my new life without my husband, I had to figure out what I needed and held on to it the best way I could.

I would suggest that when the griever encounters those who try to rush you through the grieving process, it's important that he or she remembers not to let other people impose. However, if you value the opinion of some and are open to suggestions, then that would not be an imposition.

For those who have faith, I believe that the saying, "Let go and let God," is good advice to adhere to. I've made peace with those unanswered questions by talking to my husband, writing to him in a journal, listening to what I hear in my heart, and paying attention to my dreams. Eventually, you will see the light at the end of the tunnel when you get there.

Quinton Wilkes, PhD: I've had multiple experiences with loss. They have been varied, particularly as it pertains to my family of origin and my conjugal family (the family that forms when you're married). I was an only child, an only grandchild and nephew in my family. I was reared by my grandparents. My grandson, who is seven months old, is the first male child born into my family since 1941, when I was born. So having this position in my family of origin, I experienced on an intimate level the illnesses and deaths of each of the members of my immediate family.

My eldest daughter from my first marriage died suddenly from a heart attack at age thirty-five. She had no history of heart trouble and was in good physical condition, but this sudden heart attack took her away from here. I also lost my wife from my second marriage in 2007. Each of these losses was different in various ways.

We use euphemisms for the word *died*, and that in itself may be a way of minimizing the pain of loss. My grandparents raised me. My mother was a single mother who was working and going to school at the time that I was born. My father and mother separated sometime after I was born. My grandparents took me at the age of nine months from

Washington, DC, to High Point, North Carolina, where I grew up. I stayed in contact with my mother and in the summer, I would come to New York and stay with my mother and my aunts.

My grandfather was the first one in my immediate family to pass. He and my grandmother were in their late seventies, and they eventually left their ten-room house in North Carolina and moved in with one of my aunts who lived in the Bronx, New York. My second marriage lasted twenty-two years. During the course of my marriage, it was uneven. When my wife passed away from esophageal cancer, we were not on especially good terms. She kept her illness from my two daughters and me in order to protect us from the pain of knowing. She was recuperating from a surgical procedure, and she seemed to be recuperating well, but then she developed a serious infection as a result of the surgery and within two or three days, she passed away. It was quite a shock and sad, but I also had conflicted feelings because of the quality of our relationship.

Honesty is so important when working through grief. As a therapist, I understand grief as a highly individualized process; however, individuals should allow themselves to experience the whole range of feelings, and they should try not to suppress the grief. When people say, "You shouldn't allow yourself to prolong the grief," or, "Come on now, she's been gone for a year or year and a half, pick yourself up, dust yourself off, and get on with your life," one must remember that grief feelings are natural human feelings, and people should allow themselves to feel those feelings.

Sometimes we need help with this process and that can be from a friend, family, bereavement groups, and professionals such as individual therapists, group therapy, and family therapy for an entire family who has lost a loved one. Groups that are specifically dedicated toward helping members of the group work through grief and bereavement can be very helpful. There is individual and group psychotherapy and all of these possibilities are very helpful. Grieving alone can be a tough process and probably can interfere with the natural process of grief and may prolong and complicate the process.

When dealing with the pain of loss, one must allow himself or herself to experience the pain that is the real feeling associated with the loss. A lot of people try to avoid the pain by denying the pain, drinking, using drugs, shopping, or various other tactics that help to mask the pain. The pain can be quite intense, and it is important to feel the pain. Even though it can be quite intense, you will learn that it won't kill you or incapacitate you. Many people have the fear that it will overtake them and will be so unbearable, but it is important to allow oneself to feel it as soon as possible and not be afraid of it.

One should also be able to express the pain verbally and be able to share their feelings with others, for example, clergy or family members. People will often speak with a minister or priest before they seek professional therapy. Bereavement groups are excellent because sometimes family and friends really don't understand. It is important to know that grief and the grieving process is highly, highly individualized, and no one can tell anyone how or how long one should grieve.

Freud wrote a book entitled, *Mourning and Melancholia* (melancholia is an unhealthy kind of grieving). There is a rule of thumb that many people experience grief in a tangible way for a year or two, but when a person is experiencing intense grief after five or six years, and it's disrupting other parts of his or her life, then that gets into what's called complicated grief or melancholia, and that's when professional help is really needed.

Grief is one of those emotions or situations that other people don't deal with very well. People who care about us hate to see us suffer, so oftentimes in order to relieve themselves of the suffering that they experience when they see you suffer, they will try to cut it off by saying things like, "Come on, you pull yourself together," or, "Now, now, no tears," and other platitudes of that sort.

Religious and spiritual beliefs can also be very helpful, because you believe that there is something much more powerful, profound, larger, and wiser than yourself. Believing in an afterlife or everlasting life or that our loved one is in a better place is also beneficial. It's important that those who are grieving recognize that grieving is very individualized, and we all have our own ways of experiencing grief. Some of these ways are influenced by our cultural backgrounds and religious beliefs.

Getting through grief is easier said than done. Sometimes when someone dies and there are unresolved conflicts and ambivalence and unfinished business, it can be difficult to resolve them once the person has passed away. Thus, like I said before, talking to someone, either a group where the individuals have suffered a similar loss, clergy, or a professional can help to guide you through the difficult feelings. They can encourage you through most of the difficulty you encounter when facing grief and loss.

We can be brave by facing the full range of feelings that we feel. Sometimes the most difficult feelings are not just the sadness, sense of loss, and the aloneness, but the anger. Often these are forbidden emotions, so allowing oneself to experience the feelings, whatever they are, and allowing one to try to explore the feelings, meanings, and where they might be coming from will help us to move forward through the process. Sometimes these feelings bring out losses we've experienced that can conjure up deep-rooted feelings related to feeling abandoned and left.

One can continue the relationship with a spouse who has passed away through memories, reflections, and talking about the lost loved one with other people who knew him or her. And of course, we have the internalized representation of that person: how they looked, their idiosyncrasies, etc. These are all ways of continuing a relationship with the person. Now, there's the question of whether or not one can actually experience the spirit of someone who has passed on, and this can be secular or nonsecular. Some believe that the spirit of the person can return. My grandfather told me once that he didn't believe in ghosts, but he did believe in wandering spirits. There is the possibility that if a person isn't at peace, then he or she may not pass into the next plane, and his or/her spirit can stick around. So yes, I believe that one can continue the relationship with a lost loved one through recollections, remembrances, and memories.

Through my experience of loss, I gained maturity, and I think there's something psychological about that. It is said that a man doesn't truly become a man until he loses his father. In my family of origin, I felt that my family had done well by me, and I had done well by them. When my second wife and I first got married, we were deeply in love for a significant part of our relationship, and then we began to have difficulties. But even with the difficulties, we still had love for each other, although there was a mixture of other feelings there.

The loss of my daughter, my wife, and my grandparents were all difficult and painful, but the loss of my grandparents was the most difficult because they were my surrogate parents. This was my first experience with death, and I probably experienced some anticipatory grief, so I would consider this loss my greatest. I had had very healthy and good relationships with my family of origin. I felt that I was able to be at the best of my ability when they were going through their final illnesses. So, I had that final peace of mind that I'd done my best.

Barbara B.: My husband and love of my life, Tony, was diagnosed with lung cancer. We sought treatment and pursued it from September, 2007, through March, 2009, when he passed away, leaving me absolutely devastated. We had been together twenty-four hours a day, seven days a week for the past nine years of my retirement, working in and enjoying an antique business. We were also together 24/7 during his cancer treatment, and I just thought of it as a new stage or new reality—the way we would live from now on, traveling to and from the hospital for treatments and emergencies. I was adjusted to it and had convinced myself that we could go on like this for a very long time—of course, always praying and hoping for the miraculous cure. When he died sixteen months later, I was in shock.

He'd been getting pneumonia more frequently (after each chemo session) and finally, the doctor said because of the pneumonias, he could no longer treat him, and he was sending him to hospice. We were both in shock because hospice meant the end! But then I told Tony, and I convinced myself that it was because of the pneumonia, and if he built himself up in hospice, he would come home. For three days, he ate everything on his plate and then some. He seemed strong and alert. The doctor had given him six weeks, but he passed away in six days.

I was unprepared. The next few days were a blur of preparations—buying the cemetery plot, arranging for the wake, the funeral, the playing of taps at the grave site, and the burial—all of which I did in a surreal haze. I did not feel pain or grief; I did not feel anything. I just knew what I had to do to the best of my ability: to give Tony the best wake, funeral, and burial I could. I put together a nice picture board with highlights of his life and arranged for a nice post-burial dinner for family and friends. I was pleased that he would have been pleased.

And then came the shock and emptiness and the feeling of helplessness and hopelessness. I felt like my life was over and that I should have been buried with him (the way they did in some ancient civilizations when they buried the wife with the husband when he died). I did not consider killing myself, but I did not want to live. I remember lying in bed and wishing and hoping that I would not wake up in the morning. However, I did live, and I did phone the grief facilitator at Sloan-Kettering who listened to me cry for a full hour once a week for the next month and a half until the bereavement group that she so masterfully put together got started. I thought I was not emotionally ready for a group yet, but she convinced me that I was. For that, I am grateful, extremely grateful.

I believe that people should grieve any way they want to; whatever works for them. It's an individual experience for each person, and each person will treat it differently. No one can understand how you feel (except someone who has experienced the same thing, like my unique bereavement group).

I have had well-meaning friends say, "I know how you feel, and I remember how I felt when my mother died." While I also lost my father and mother at ages forty-five years and fifty-seven years, and although it was a tremendous loss, it was not anything like having the inside of your heart ripped out and being left with an overwhelming void. So, no one could tell me as they tried to say things like, "Don't wear black," "Don't think about his suffering because it will depress you," "You should get out more."

I would suggest seeking a counselor if one feels really depressed. Otherwise, or, in addition, I definitely suggest a bereavement group. Look for one that is narrowed, as much as possible, to the specific circumstances of your experience, for example, husband, or parents, or child, etc. (narrowed even more by your relationship to the deceased). Look for a group in the same category as you and even better if it can be narrowed down to the same circumstance of loss, if possible.

The closer you can narrow it down, the greater the bonding with your group will be. The more you identify with each other, the greater the healing benefit will be. My bereavement group is the only place I feel a real connection of understanding and compassion. It helped me to advance my grief because they were struggling out of the same heartache, and we progressed through it together.

I believe that someone who is about to embark on the grieving process should do it sooner than later. Pushing it away to avoid the problem will not work. In my opinion, it just will not be ignored and can possibly manifest itself through health issues or psychological issues that you may not readily recognize or admit as being related.

When I think about what I've gained through this loss, it's strength. Strength to live through the terrifying sense that there is now a tremendous hole in your heart, a pervading void in your life, and you don't know how to go on. Strain to reach out in your pain, strain to subconsciously try to seek out distractions to help your mind to focus on something other than your loved one and your loss. For some it's work. For others who are retired, it's friends or church or charity work—anything that allows you to focus your mind on something other than your grief.

Things began to take a turn for me when one evening, I phoned the local pizza parlor for delivery. It was 8:00 p.m., there was a lot of noise in the background, and the owner distractedly said, "Call back tomorrow," and hung up. Well, I was hungry tonight, so I left my house in what had now become my uniform: black T-shirt and black slacks, which I had endowed with magical powers. I felt the black clothing comforted me by making me feel enveloped and protected from the world (despite the admonishments of family and friends that "no one wears black anymore").

I walked two blocks and peered into the glass door of the pizza parlor. There appeared to be a party in the rear. I stood outside wondering if I could still order something at the counter when a tall, blonde woman, who had been standing outside smoking, asked me if there was anything wrong. I explained, and she told me she was with one group in the back. She said that they were all friends who came here weekly for dinner and karaoke, and she invited me to join them and order dinner at her table.

I was stunned and wanted to say no, but something beyond myself propelled me to say, "Okay." I remember thinking that I could always excuse myself and leave if I couldn't go through with it. She brought me to her table and introduced me to her friends, men and women. I ordered. Several people at other tables got up to sing. I panicked when the words of a song made my eyes fill up with tears, but I cast my eyes down while wondering how to escape without making a scene. Eventually, it passed, and I regained my composure, only to have it happen again with another song. This time, I felt better able to handle it since I was not "discovered" during the first episode. Although I had to dab away some tears with my fingers, I was able to stay till my new friend walked me home.

It became a regular thing that I looked forward to, and I met a lot of nice people. It took my mind off my loss on Fridays, and also on the day before when I had to plan to wear something other than "black." I also removed my wedding bands so no one would ask me about my spouse, which would definitely set off a river of tears. This was my first breath of regular air and what would become my journey from the land of grief.

After eight months, things changed (as we all know too well that they can). The dinner group broke up for one reason or another, and the whole karaoke thing came to an end. I occasionally bump into these people, and it contributes to making my neighborhood a more welcoming environment.

After having had this experience or respite from my grieving, I was able to start putting other pieces of my life back together. After months of closing myself off from most human contact except for my bereavement group (eight weekly sessions), I think God intervened. There is a saying that goes sort of like this: some people come into your life for a reason, some for a season, and some for a lifetime; embrace them all!

Kyndell A. Reid, Esq.: In 1975 at the age of seventeen, my mother died of cancer. I was in my senior year of high school and was about to graduate. I was the only child of a single-parent home. It all started when my mother was coming home from work one day and stated, "I tripped on the curb." I didn't think much about it. Then, it happened again, and she repeated, "I tripped on a curb again, and I can't raise my ankle." She went to the foot doctor, and he told her that nothing was wrong with her foot or her leg.

A few months earlier, my mother had started getting headaches. The doctor scheduled her immediately for tests at Columbia Presbyterian Hospital, in New York City. After the tests, it was discovered that she had a brain tumor. From February to April, it was back and forth to the hospital for radiation treatments. The brain tumor was finally dissolved, and she was able to lift her foot and walk again. However, her blood count continued to drop, and the white blood cells were eating up the red blood cells and the doctors did not know why. In May, she had to be admitted into the hospital for further testing.

I didn't understand. I knew the brain tumor had been dissolved, and I never associated a brain tumor with cancer. At that time, cancer was a hush-hush word and was never mentioned to me during my mother's short illness; before that, she had never been sick a day in her life. In June, the doctors operated, and I was told there was nothing further that they could do. From my recollection, the doctors said that once they opened her up, they found that the cancer had spread. It was then I was told she had pancreatic cancer.

During those last weeks, after the operation, my mother was in extraordinary pain. Although I would go to the hospital, I could not bear to see her in such agony. It was about 1:00 a.m. on July 9, that I received a call from my grandfather. He told me that my mother had passed away … I almost let out a sigh of relief. My mother was no longer in agony, no longer in pain, no longer suffering. So, in my mind, I decided that my mother was now free, and I had to go on with my life. At that point, I was only concerned about my mother and her pain, not realizing that one day, I would have to deal with her loss, my grief, and my suffering.

The loss of my mother at a very early age was very traumatic. At seventeen, this is the time you need love, guidance, and direction about life, and you do not know who to trust. So you must learn to trust yourself, and your instincts in your life's decisions—good or bad, right or wrong.

It took me twenty years to get through the grief of the loss of my mother. During this time, I learned to laugh to keep from crying. I would say that grieving is a very personal process, and individuals need to do whatever works best for them. You must first understand that you have a loss and that grieving is part of the process. Eventually, one will find that he or she gains a certain amount of independence and a different identity as a result of the loss. I don't think that there's a limit as to how long one should grieve. Each situation is different, but it is important to allow yourself *to grieve.* No one ever imposed a timetable on my grieving process, but maybe that's because I never took the time to actually grieve the loss of my mother.

CHAPTER 15

Hope

There is a saying that time heals all wounds, but I believe that time alone doesn't heal anything; it's what you do with the time that will help us heal. Time is one of those constants in our lives, but it is an intangible. We cannot see it, hear it, touch it, or smell it, but we trust that it is there with us every step of the way. It is not unlike our shadow: always with us, but we can never touch it or feel it even though we know it is a constant in our lives. Time pushes us forward whether we like it or not. We cannot pause it even though, when we are grieving, there are many times when we will long to do so just to give ourselves a breather and to provide some relief from the excruciating pain of grief and loss.

In the beginning of our ordeal, we do not see time as our friend. We may wonder how long we will feel numb, depressed, anguished, and in a fog. Could this go on forever? Will there ever be a time when we will feel relief from this aching despair? But time gives us an opportunity to go through a natural healing process. We pass through invisible stages as we move forward. Sometimes, you might feel like you have a handle on your grief, and then a song or a picture, or seeing someone who looks like the one you've lost will trigger a deep and abiding sadness. You might even begin to feel that you've taken ten steps backward.

As you grieve, you must do many things in order to get back on the road to recovery. Initially, I found that as I entered the world of grieving (I characterize this as such because once my husband died, it was as if I slipped off the earth into another planet), it felt like I was living a parallel existence. It was as if I existed partly in the real world and partly in a surreal world that was shrouded by a gray veil of gloom, both simultaneously.

I was a walking, living, breathing dead person. That's the numb stage. The day-to-day is challenging. You find yourself enduring each day instead of living it. Each day feels like a stream of time—night to day, day to night. It's no longer hours, days, weeks, months, but one single thread of time differentiated by only the light of day and the dark of night.

However, as time goes on (and this is individual to each person), comfort will come with clarity of mind. As you begin to be able to think more clearly, stay focused, see the pinhole of light (which will enlarge as you move forward), if you give yourself permission to do so, you will find that you're enjoying life more and not just being numb in it. You must get past all of the sad thoughts and embrace the comfort you feel as you begin to reawaken and look at life in fresh new ways.

One of the things that helped me to move forward was the fact that I had a diverse community of friends. I had friends of various ages from many cultural backgrounds, and I found this fact to be critical to my recovery. Because I had managed to cultivate different friends over the years, I didn't now find myself stuck in a place, trying to construct a social life. I had had one all along that I could now tap into. That fact for me was crucial to my moving forward.

So, my longtime friends were there with support and love, while my newer friends (maybe as recent as ten years or so) were also there with love and support, but they also provided opportunities for me to get out and to do new things and participate in different social activities. They were less encumbered by family responsibilities, and they had newer and fresher ideas and were full of an energy and vitality that helped to get me as "current" as I could handle.

I didn't have grandchildren to turn my attention to or a garden to tend, and I was not encumbered by family responsibilities or a job I needed to be at every day. In some ways, I was lucky to have had the freedom to move forward without distractions. I was free to become who I was going to become without my husband by my side. I didn't have anything in my life that would distract me from dealing with my sorrow. I could consciously fight my way out of the abysmal sense of loneliness and sadness without being distracted, which could prolong my recovery process.

I soon began to see that small flicker of light at the end of the tunnel become larger. And actually without my noticing, I had begun to feel less numb and more alive. It was a gradual process, but I was ever aware of the fragility of my state of being and a newly emerging strength and feeling of being grounded. I eventually began to see that the void that my husband's passing had created in my life could be utilized by me in myriad ways. In fact, that void, that emptiness, had now become a place of hope and an opportunity to create a new path or "thing" in my life as I began to believe that there could be "life after death."

But the key here is that I never gave up. I never gave up on the fact that I could get through the sadness, the crying, the mourning, and the hollow feelings. I felt that if I held on—or in the words of one of my favorite aunts, continued to "carry on"—that I would have a breakthrough and be able to reach beyond the dark days and begin anew. And I did; suddenly I was able to do more. I was able to experience life without my life being tinged by sadness. This took many, many, months and years to achieve, but I wanted to get on with things as I followed this new road and opened a new chapter in my life.

About a year or so after my husband passed away, a colleague of mine lost her husband suddenly. I arrived at her home for the shiva, and she approached me and asked how I'd gotten from the early stages of grief to the present. I told her that I started mourning right away. She said she wanted to begin grieving immediately. She wanted to know what she could expect. I asked her how she felt now, just hours since her husband had passed. She said she felt numb, and my reply was that this was stage one.

So here was a woman who was about to grieve consciously, like me. Doing so doesn't necessarily lessen the grieving time it just keeps you aware as you begin the grieving journey. The plus side is that when there is that flicker of light at the end of your tunnel, you will recognize that as *hope*.

In the end, I have been able to see the world with new eyes filled with optimism and hope, and I feel that I have achieved my goal, which is to be able to forge a life of my own.

CHAPTER 16

How to Remember a Spouse

I believe that the best way to remember a spouse is in that person's entirety. Remember him or her in the wholeness of who he or she was. When time has passed and we are no longer in the deepest darkest days of our grief, we will think about things differently. We will come to have a new perspective on our spouse, our lives with our spouse, the memories that we created, and the life that we have without them.

There are all kinds of memorials and tributes that one can have in memory of those we have lost, but the greatest tribute is to continue to *live*. We must continue to live our lives to the best of our ability and know that if we imagine that our spouses are in a better place that they would want nothing less than for us to live the remainder of our lives with enthusiasm, happiness, and joy.

This is not an easy thing to do, and it is a progression, but in time as we adjust to our aloneness, we will find that we have a tendency to become fixed in old ideas and ways. This is our comfort zone. We should strive to look beyond our present life and be able to see the possibilities and begin to discard old ways of thinking and old habits.

This will help us to stretch our spirit as we begin to become open to all that life has to offer.

Time and energy are always evolving. Nothing on earth is fixed, and nothing remains the same day by day, minute by minute, thus we must move and grow and evolve also so that we can begin to fill the void left by the death of the husband or wife, with new ideas and experiences. Sometimes after losing a spouse, many people remain detached from their feelings; they're afraid to "go there." But it's the very act of "going there" and feeling the pain, grief, and anguish that eventually will allow you to move past the grief and into a fresh new place full of possibilities and wonder.

You may even find yourself as you move your life forward, wondering if you really would want your spouse to come back. That's because nothing is black and white. There is always that gray, and as we begin to feel better and begin to create new lives for ourselves, we will begin to know that our thoughts and feelings are complicated, and they change daily. We will also come to know that if we imagine our spouses in a "better place," they certainly wouldn't want to come back to earth and, therefore, it's okay for us to continue on and to find happiness in new experiences.

Being strong is not what I consider honoring one's spouse. A person can become so strong and removed from the pain of the loss that he or she becomes brittle, which in itself is another form of fragility. One can become locked in a "zone," neither fully alive nor dead but like an emotional zombie. We must deal with ourselves with compassion and empathy.

If you imagine your partner to be in a place where he or she is no longer encumbered by earthly judgments, opinions, values, and mores, then know that he or she is rooting for you because you are still here and life is full of amazing, wondrous, and astounding experiences. Your spouse wants you to move forward and take advantage of your life and be one with it. He or she wants you to know that joy, peace, and love abound. I suggest we honor a lost spouse by doing the work to rekindle your spirit after you have mourned and grieved. There is no greater way to pay tribute to the life of the one whom we once were partnered with than to continue to live with enthusiasm, purposefulness, faith, hope, and love.

I enjoy my new life now. It was a long road to this place, but I do cherish this experience. I know that my husband and I were meant to have shared our journey. I am grateful for his presence in my life and will always love and cherish him and our life together. Although I wish that my husband were here with me, I also know that the life that I have now is my life, not our life. We had our life the way it was together, and the life I'm living now with enthusiasm is the one that I'm supposed to have on my own. This is how I'm remembering my husband, and this is how anyone can best remember his or her spouse ... by being brave in a new world.

EPILOGUE

I often think about the bravery and courage that my husband exhibited in the darkest days of his battle with pancreatic cancer. I believe that those qualities are the hallmarks of his legacy that will endure with those who knew him, especially me.

I have become brave in my new world, and I know that as I continue with my life and as I fulfill my own purpose, I'm also fulfilling my destiny. Chuck was a part of that destiny, but I've discovered that there are many experiences that one can have before one's life is done. I wrote this book to share my story with the hope that it will assist all those who find themselves on a grieving journey. My wish is that in your darkest hour, you can be reassured that, after a time, there is life after death as you begin to create a new life of your own.

ACKNOWLEDGMENTS

I wish to thank all of my friends and family who have supported me throughout this writing process. Without my "community of saints," I would not have had the encouragement, support, empathy, and love that have sustained me these past three years that I have been working on this project. I want to give a special thanks to Ken Lipper, who was the first one that I approached about writing about grieving the loss of his dear friend, my husband, Chuck Loftin. He encouraged me and helped me to set forth a vision as I embarked on this writing journey.

I also want to thank the Rev. Dr. Arnold Isidore Thomas who supported me enthusiastically throughout this entire process. He was truly my guiding light, offering support and spiritual insight. My dear friends Brenda Spears, Lisa Peterson, Donna White, and Carol St. Ange were the "girls" to call on when I needed my spirits lifted. They gave me love and encouragement and did so with patience and without judgment.

My family stood by me in my darkest days: My mother, Dorothy Broady; my siblings, Marie, Anthony, and Emil; and my son, Karim, gave me the strength that I needed, which replaced the strength that I had once received from Chuck. They encouraged me and helped me to move forward, and for that I am most appreciative. My brothers were very kind to me, offering me support and love along my grieving journey. My cousin Betty Burgess-Walker was at my side in the early days after my loss. She and her husband, my cousin, Clint Walker, were pillars of strength for me and helped to distract me with myriad activities when I went to their town in order to get away from New York early on after my husband's death.

My cousins Louis Martin and his wife, Caroline, would send me cards while Chuck was ill, letting me know that they were thinking of me and Chuck and praying on our behalf. My cousins Frenchie and Joyce Robinson would call periodically or send us e-mails to check up on their cousins and to let us know that they were praying for us and keeping us in their thoughts. I received support and love from friends and family; my sister, Marie, who was so helpful to me early on; and so many others, including Ahlilah Longmire who guided my initial steps into the world of writing and publishing.

I send a special thank-you to dear friend Toni Willard who always offered an enthusiastic word of encouragement. I also want to thank a special group of friends whom I met along the way, who really helped me get through the grief that I was experiencing over the loss of my husband, Chuck. They are: Angel, Kathy, Liz, Bonnie, Krissy, Julia, Navya, and Rain. They helped me to cross uncharted waters in my search for peace and solace and the rediscovery of myself. Without them I would never have been able to go forth and carve out a future for myself.

I also want to extend a special thank-you to Laura Harris, Robin Walton, Dr. Ellen Bialo, and my husband's sweet sister, Cathy Bridges. In addition, the wonderful folks at Brick Run Sports Physical Therapy in New York City kept my body mobile and my spirits lifted. Thank you to them and especially Gurjeet Chadha, clinical director.

And last, but not least, I want to thank from the bottom of my heart my wonderful friends, the Journeyettes, who are the members of my bereavement group. They are: Phil, Barbara, Carol, Dan, Donna, and Margaret. We began this journey together connected by our deep grieving and losses. We were always there for each other with love, compassion, patience, encouragement, hope, and good cheer.

CPSIA information can be obtained at www.ICGtesting.com
Printed in the USA
LVOW07s0253301214

420865LV00001B/72/P